I0094145

Why I Stayed

Memoirs from the Tropics

Licualawinq Writers

Itchy Emu Press

Itchy Emu Publishers

Copyright

Contents

Introduction

Dear Readers,

This project began as a challenge issued by Licualawinq member and author Ken Allen after he delivered a talk to the group on publishing through IngramSpark and Amazon. He suggested we create a collaborative work for him to use for a 'hands on' publishing demonstration for members. The result is an insight into life in Queensland's Wet Tropics from eleven writers aged from their twenties to their eighties. We hope you enjoy reading your way through these pages—you may find yourself laughing, crying, sweating, and squirming as you are drawn into true tales of love, adventure, courage, wisdom gained, inspiration, devastation and resilience, connection to the land, green and scene changes, and wildlife encounters.

Most contributors to this volume have been traditionally and independently published many times, and for a couple it is their first time seeing their own by-line. Licualawinq aims to nurture Cassowary Coast writers from their first words on a page. It provides a friendly forum for new and experienced writers of all genres, a safe place to stretch creative wings and receive honest feedback and encouragement.

We thank Ken for inspiring us to share our stories and poems, providing his photographs for the cover, and guiding us on this self-publishing journey.

Jacque Duffy
Coordinator Licualawinq.

Heart of Lightness

By Cassandra Smith

"So, how did you end up here?" inquired my lunch guest, a new teacher to the far north. I guessed she was asking why on God's green earth would anyone be living in a small town in the far north of Queensland when they seemed like a relatively normal person.

Possible reasons ran through my head. Is it that there are fewer cars? Is it that the stars are brighter? Or there's less pollution? Fewer people? That someone will offer you a spot on their camp site because you arrived late? People are kinder? More considerate? You are known? You have the space to breathe? It's all of those things but none of these is the reason I stayed.

Real locals will know you are not from here. They can trace back antecedents for most family names and will joyfully do so when trying to place someone. The question of why one stays is something I've heard often in my 14 years here. They go alongside, "You're not from around here, are you?" and "Where are you from?" Some refugees from the south do not like to acknowledge that we came from elsewhere. There's a whiff that there may be something 'not-quite-right' with us. That we couldn't cut it in the 'real world', AKA the city, so we had to flee to the north. Since COVID, which in tiny Innisfail meant little change to the daily routine, there have been more people fleeing from southern climes to the warm and sunny tropics to escape not just the colder weather, but also the mandatory lockdowns. They have benefitted from the much lower prices for housing here but in doing so pushed up prices for locals.

When I came here in 2008, I had to confront the old stereotype. I wasn't shipwrecked like Eliza Fraser in far north Queensland, a fish out of water, unable to communicate with the locals and unexpectedly teaching polite phrases to an 'uncivilised' society. No, I came by choice.

In the 1980s in Sydney, I was called a 'banana bender' for the first time. Well, it's true that the far north is the home of rural industries such as sugarcane and bananas. But, even to someone from the state capital Brisbane, who is aware of these unfair stereotypes, to head to the far north was likened to entering the heart of darkness. This image is not helped by films such as Wolf Creek. The north of Australia is often perceived as miles of deathly highway where serial killers can lurk. One is more likely to die of boredom on the highway though, than of an opportunistic serial killer. Staying awake on that long stretch between Rocky and Mackay is the real killer.

You've probably noticed the way it mirrors the stereotypical way the American southern states, the Confederate ones, are regarded by their northern 'Union' cousins in the United States. America's South is hot, sultry, and stereotyped as the backward home of slavery and inequity. Of course, in the southern hemisphere it's flipped; in Australia, the further north you go in Queensland toward the tip, the closer to the Equator and the hotter and more humid the temperature. Fewer services, fewer golden arches, fewer people. More roads, and less traffic. I guess there are many consonances. Like many parts of Australia, Queensland has huge homesteads taken by squatters, thanks to Terra Nullius—the lie that meant Australia was a blank slate—or had no owners. The far north has had its slaves, the Kanakas, taken from their islands in the Pacific and forced to work on plantations. Young Aboriginal women from the stolen generation were put in service, but not just in the far north. It was also the site of resistance against colonial rule at Battle Creek for example. And home to many Italian immigrants who were rounded up during WWII as potential spies. The far north of Queensland, was, and I would argue, still is, the home of the deep unconscious for Australians.

Some of the disdain we reserve for ourselves is a holdover from a white colonial past—the vestigial tail of British class snobbery that regarded those from the Antipodes as being uncouth and uncultured, at the very least. There is the related notion that Australians had to visit the 'Mother Country' as a rite of passage, a trope especially true of writers and artists of the 20th century. This was very real in the 70s for our Clive James and our Germaine Greer, a few of those who had to swim beyond the small pool to fully unfurl their creative wings. In our connected, global world, this notion now seems out of date. But the cultural baggage persists, lurking in our DNA or our dark, northern subconscious.

As one travels north, the temperature rises to similar and beyond the southern Australian states, but besides the certainty of regular tropical rainfall and potential cyclones, it's the humidity—which one must experience to truly understand—that is most notable. The further north you travel, as the temperature and humidity rise, the clothes come off and inhibitions alongside them. As Freud would have noted had he been Australian—it's hard to have hang-ups when you're wearing a pair of shorts—and thongs I'd add. Some long summer days it seems the unbearable heat can only really be staunched by a cold alcoholic beverage. To numb consciousness. It seems somehow more permissible. The ocean and pools are a luke-warm bath instead of a refreshing respite. Laid low during the midday fug, one lolls in the drenching humidity until forced to seek shelter in the aircon inside, blocking out the environment completely.

ele

A fresh start or on the run anyone?

The rule of law becomes notional. Pre-COVID, foreign male backpackers walked about bare-chested, glorying in the unfamiliar, glaring hot sunshine. I repressed the urge to shout at them out the window of my car "Put a shirt on!" and settled for a shake of my head and a muttered "Backpackers". Or sprawling at the local beauty spots frying scarlet in the sun with twin moons exposed to the world separated by their 'thongs'. I shake my head; they've never heard of melanoma.

People heading north have been known to 'go troppo' under the illusion they are escaping their past, leaving civilisation's city scape far behind in the rear-view mirror along with cultural norms such as remaining clothed in public. Occasionally a story surfaces of someone on the run from the law for years who eventually gets uncovered in some far north locale—where it's perceived laws are lax and time has somehow stopped. Or that people will be more likely to let you be. A recent case was Graham Potter, wanted by police since 2010, on the run from conspiracy to murder charges in Melbourne. He was arrested in 2022 in the small mountain township of Ravenshoe, a two-hour drive west of Cairns where he had been living in squalid conditions in a shack. It was reported that he had last been seen in Tully in 2010—two years after my arrival.

This is the territory I was to end up in, deep. I didn't leave behind my clothes, but I had to borrow $100 from my sister to buy suitable apparel for my new job as a teacher.

—— *ele* ——

"Don't you miss the city?" inquired my new friend.

When I lived in inner-city Brisbane in my twenties, I felt oppressed by the pressure to conform to a subcultural group most often signalled by dressing in the way of that group. When I was a student at the University of Queensland in the early 90s, the Country Road brand was a marker of middle-classness. It seemed to be emblazoned on everyone's shirt and bag. It told people, "I am part of this tribe". The message was, "I can spend $50 on a T-shirt." I wasn't one of those people. I'd come from north of Brisbane, Deception Bay, a housing commission area. My parents worked at the Golden Circle cannery in Northgate until my mother got pregnant with my younger brother. I was the first from my family to go to university. I knew one other student from my high school. It was part of my getting of wisdom to see the privileged classes who'd gone to the prestige schools, who lived in the colleges, which I couldn't even entertain the idea of, and who all seemed to know one another. At first, I tried to fit in, but I soon realised that even if I wanted to be like them, I never could be. I did notice eventually that many went wild with their first taste of freedom. I was a little more prepared for having to look after myself and expected to work.

In my Journalism course I met a girl with gorgeous long curly dark russet locks and a wide mouth, who told me about getting a frock made for the races at Ascot. "You have to, Darling! It's race day!" drawled she. No one would be caught dead wearing the same frock twice! Despite the fact I had my $312 student payment budgeted to the last cent, we became friends. I admitted to her my father was an alcoholic, like it explained something important about me. "Isn't everyone's?" she mocked. I supposed she was right. We parted ways after she made moves on my boyfriend of the time.

Most offspring of young professionals were studying professions themselves while I was studying Arts. I laughed aloud when I saw scrawled in black Nikko above the toilet roll dispenser in the Forgan Smith law library toilets: "Arts degrees—take one please". At last, I understood! Here, being a teacher was considered very low on the totem pole.

I tried living with some girls in St Lucia. We were kind to each other, but we were clearly from different worlds. I found a share house in West End, a ferry ride across the river from St Lucia. This was before the arrival of the smart sleek City Cats. Back then the ferries were still the quaint little old tug-boat style. And so, I became a West End girl. It was there I found my people among other misfits and outsiders.

"Dyke city!" screamed the graffiti on the bridge where Dornoch Terrace crossed over Boundary Street. In the early 90s West End was a haven for lesbians while Newfarm, next to The Valley, was considered the ancestral home of gay men. I moved into a beautiful old white Queenslander on the river with my ex's sister Maria and a pair of sisters. One morning Maria unkindly snapped a photo of me exiting the toilet, which was attached to the outside of the house. I was a skinny deer caught in the headlights. I wore a red checked flannel shirt and purple thermal pants, which I'd bought at a local op shop and dyed. I was a naïve 21. I remember them breaking to me the fact that one of my housemates was a lesbian and the penny dropping. Maria moved out and more lesbians moved in until I was the only hetero left in the house.

"We'll make a lesbian out of you yet!" they'd threaten.

And, "You may as well go out with a girl, the guys you go out with are like girls".

I was annoyed by this but to be fair, I did cut my hair short, West End style, and let my armpit and leg hair grow long—I was an arts student after all. I did a feminist philosophy subject and started going to rallies with friends. I shopped at op shops, became vegetarian, rode a bicycle as transport and wore whatever I liked. I was shocked when Paul Keating was ousted from government but even though a new conservative dawn was rising, my life still seemed rich with possibility.

I finished my degree with Honours in English, so virtually unemployable, but emboldened by Paul Keating's forged connections with our Asian neighbours, I went to Japan for a year to teach English. Suddenly robbed of rich conversation, I scribbled incessantly in journals and wrote fervid letters to friends.

I came back to Brisbane surprised to find everything had changed. All my friends had moved on and I still had to find my way. I had no family or other connections for a leg or foot up. And I now had pretensions to write. While living in Japan I'd realised that comparatively Australia had a vibrant youth culture and now I wanted to contribute. I volunteered and worked a variety of shows at community radio station 4ZZZ, which started at University of Queensland in the 70s and was then located in the Valley. I contributed to the Movie Show, the women's show, drive-times, news headlines, and had my own show at 12-2pm on a Friday night I called 'The Pink Room'. I announced there under a nom de guerre, Gigi, and began the show with a bump and grind number from Twin Peaks by Angelo Badalamenti. At the same time, I wrote for street magazine 'Rave', interviewing bands and reviewing gigs, films, plays and festivals. I interviewed touring bands that were releasing albums and local musicians. Because I was working at 4ZZZ, I ended up on the punk round, which no one self-respecting was interested in at Rave. The pay was $25 a review and $30 per interview, so it was not what one could call a real career. After a few years of learning the job, I helped launch a pop culture magazine called 'Schmoozer' on a literal shoestring as the assistant editor. I'd learnt about the realities of how music journalism was akin to PR. You interviewed bands the record companies were promoting. They sent media releases and set up interviews and gave publications 'product' to review. By writing about them you were promoting their product, the band, and selling units for their record label. The philosophy behind Schmoozer was simple: going to gigs gratis and cadging free CDs just for writing about it. I was good at it. I remember being called upon to cajole our printer to print our first edition even though we hadn't paid the full amount. They printed the edition.

And schmooze we did. I had fun, made friends, and brushed shoulders with some interesting artists, but I wasn't feeling fulfilled. I felt frustrated, as though I'd missed out on something, like my life was just out of reach. After a few years I also realised that being on the fringes of the music industry was not such a healthy lifestyle choice. At the same time, I'd made some not-so-stellar choices. I was reaching out to grasp the golden ring on the great merry-go-round of life, but I was never quite catching it, instead I was getting motion sickness.

One day I woke up. Suddenly, I was no longer in my 20s. I was a well-read barista with an honours degree in English. My world no longer felt so rich in possibilities. I was starting to feel like ripe fruit rotting on the vine. I'd joked about extending my adolescence into my 30s, but really, it's not much of a joke. I wince as I re-read my journals from that time. The girl who wrote them seems lost and desperate. She was angry because the promise of her youth had come to nothing. She wanted so much to feel loved and fill the caustic emptiness that she chased away anything resembling it. She believed in nothing, was self-obsessed, vain, and too interested in how others saw her. I badly needed something to change.

ele

Tick. Tock. Tick. Tock.

My ticking clock for a uterus seemed to be moving me of its own accord.

'Girls can do anything!' was my mindset as a girl. A product of then prime minister Gough Whitlam's programs to encourage girls, I decided at around 10 years of age that I would have a career, and then at 35, I would settle down and have a child. Turns out I'd left my run a tad late. By 2008, I had been single for three years and despaired of ever finding someone compatible. Or starting a family.

It was time to put away childish things. I took stock of my career. Holding a Bachelor of Arts with a major in English, like many arts students before me, I made the sensible choice to do a Graduate Diploma in teaching. It may sound trite, but I also wanted to redeem myself. I added up 10 years of wasted time and vowed to myself, and whatever gods were listening, that I'd offer service for the same amount of time. It's now been 14 years.

ele

Letting go

Since coming north, I feel more myself if that makes sense. I had to travel far to realise that I'm not like anyone else, nor do I try or long to be anyone else. It became a place where I could forgive myself for the all the wrong turns I'd made in the past.

I finally finished my Grad Dip., achieved a Rating 1 and applied to schools in Brisbane. My first job offer was at Brisbane's only

Moslem school. I knocked back the job. Quite the idealist, I wanted to teach in public schools because, as a product of the public school system, I believed in the amazing transformative power of education. Getting no traction in Brisbane, I took my sister's advice to strike out up north. She'd done it successfully as a speech pathologist and transplanted her family to Yeppoon in central Queensland in the 90s. The far north of Queensland was, and still is, crying out for more professionals. It sometimes takes weeks to see a GP or months or a plane trip to Brisbane to see a specialist. My sister had made a good life for her family outside the metropolitan area, so thus encouraged I applied for a job at Trinity Beach, north of Cairns.

Instead, I got the phone call offering me a job to teach at a State High School south of Cairns.

"You're going where?" inquired my best friend, at whose place I was gratefully ensconced for my second stint. She'd indulged my student penury much longer than anyone else and I still love her for it to this day.

I checked it out online. I discovered that it was a farming town of about 11000 people beside the Bruce Highway, a couple of hours north of Townsville and a couple of hours south of Cairns. The main industries were bananas and sugar cane farming and like many north Queensland towns, there was a local sugar mill.

"Oh look! It has the most UFO sightings in Australia!"

We pondered the reason for this phenomenon over dinner.

"I think they smoke too much whacky tobacky they grow up there," suggested one friend.

"Nah, they can see the sky more up there because there's no lights at night." said another.

Considering the size of the town I gave up on the idea of finding a partner. I gave up on men. I resolved to my mum, "The students will be my kids". I was to discover this was the best thing I could have ever done.

On the surface, I came to get a job. To teach. To change my life. In retrospect it probably saved my life. I thought myself an adult as I got on my flight to Cairns, but now I see I was just a very old adolescent. I didn't expect what I was to discover about myself.

—— *ele* ——

Teaching at a regional state high school was no picnic.
"I'm not a miracle worker!" I told my Head of Department hotly after a few months. I was in way out of my depth and despite working hard, I was not successful there. I didn't discover until I got there that the classes I was to teach were the classes of the learning support teacher. The teacher who was trained to work with students with significant needs. Further, they streamed classes, a practice I had been taught was wrong in my university course. I was given 10 F&G. These were the bottom two streamed classes. Curriculum to classroom or C2C resources, which supplied teachers with classwork ready for the classroom, were not yet available. Like many regional schools, there was a revolving door of teachers who came for their three years of service then left. There were no resources on the school intranet for these classes. My job was to create units of work, lessons, and manage the aberrant behaviour of the least literate students in the cohort. The attitude of my colleagues was somewhere between 'sink or swim' or 'as I have suffered, so shall you!' My practicum experiences at two elite private schools in Brisbane had in no way prepared me for this. The pungent smell of mould perfumed the staff room and all the classrooms. I had to search around the staff room to find scraps of resources to photocopy and create resources for which I only yet had rudimentary skills.
"You can't copy that!" One of the experienced teachers in the department said as she grabbed the booklet she had caught me copying. My mouth gaped open trying to make words like a fish out of water. I wish I had known enough to challenge her at the time. Instead, I cried hot tears of frustration and shame. She was wrong. Resources made for school do not belong to the teacher, they belonged to Education Queensland.

"I have to eat!" I wailed after I broke a tooth and realised there was no way to see a dentist at short notice here. I had to beg the Head of Department to let me go to Cairns so I could attend a dental appointment. She had little time for me. She'd taken one look at me in my grey skinny jeans and pink camo canvas shoes and dismissed me. She didn't even bother to do it subtly. I was suffering a terrible hangover from my going away party the previous evening, so perhaps she was right in her estimation of me at the time.

"If I want someone to stay, they will stay!" I overheard her say darkly toward the end of my contract. I was not asked to stay. It wasn't all bad though. I made friends with other beginning teachers and while there I was mentored by a kindly older teacher who was doing a contract and had the patience to work with me to create resources and showed me how to navigate the class in front of you with grace. She showed me true collegiality.

Love finds a way

Every woman completing her Grad Dip. in my year put on weight so, with fitness in mind, I returned to playing squash after a 'short' 13-year break. In Brisbane, over the years many squash courts had closed due to rising real estate values. This trend finally hit far north Queensland and the Innisfail courts have since shut the doors. But on my first night at the local squash courts, I discovered two things: that I could no longer serve forehand and that I had met my future husband. We talked about our families—we were both the middle of six children, and we both loved sushi. He was kind, reserved, and attentive and I instantly had a warm feeling about him. It didn't hurt that he was the best player there and he also showed me how to serve backhand instead of forehand and saved my game. Our first date began at squash, turned into a Thai dinner at Mission Beach and then a romantic walk along Wongaling Beach. He showed me around the beautiful sights of

FNQ. He took me for a weekend at the Sheraton in Port Douglas. In the lagoon he held me aloft in his arms like I was something precious. I was hooked.

He won me over with the beauty of the tropics. We visited the Boulders at Babinda, the Tableland lakes and waterfalls, Hinchinbrook Island, Josephine Falls, Golden Hole, Cardwell, Etty Bay, Mission Beach and Bramston Beach. I learnt how the lush green rainforests and the beautiful fresh cold waterholes of the Boulders and Josephine provided a natural respite from the heat. Every weekend and afternoon we would go somewhere for a cold swim.

ele

I checked again. The two pink lines were clear and definite. My heart beat even faster than before. All the signs were there. Nausea, faintness, hunger. I was pregnant. My situation looked desperate. I was pregnant, in an unfamiliar place, with no job, no savings and a new partner who was used to being single. But I felt strangely content and the beginning of a growing resolve. I was having a baby! My future husband took it as well as any man who had resigned himself to the bachelor life. As I was not asked to extend my contract at the state high school, my future husband suggested I look to Good Counsel College, the Catholic school where he'd gone. At the time I had a Myspace page with horoscopes on the side. Mine kept saying, "May good counsel be yours". I applied and spent an hour being interviewed by Al Webb the principal, and parish priest Father Frank. This was significant, as my previous principal could not spare five minutes for me. Al Webb and Father Frank were both very kind and considerate and asked me questions about my faith and my experience, which I answered honestly. They were not bothered that I professed an interest in Buddhism rather than Catholicism. They only cared that I was open to the faith. I did not mention that I was pregnant, and I was offered the job. For the first six months I wore a scarf as artfully as I could to hide my growing bump. But soon I was fooling no one.

—ele—

Being of service
I firmly believe every woman needs to be financially independent in order to live happily. My job has played a huge part in my life. I don't like to say vocation, because although I had thought about being a teacher as a child, I hadn't set my mind on it and I don't think I'm the best teacher in the world. But I did feel needed here and as if I'd been called to this place to do it. I was fortunate to be able to teach senior classes straight away and I felt I was doing a good job for my students. I was busy but I felt challenged, alive, and vital. I got involved in regional panels for reviewing student work, became a head of department and learnt a lot. So, I suppose that does sound like a vocation. I'm very grateful for the opportunities I have had because of living regionally—to learn my trade and become involved in a wider sense.

—ele—

One thing we agree upon here: "It's a great place to raise kids".
It takes great heroism to be a working mother. I tip my hat to all the working mothers out there. Having a child to be present for, who needs you, is the toughest job ever. They see you after work after the façade slips. I have only one child, but I know what it is to take one hat off on the way home, then put on the other. The cooking, cleaning, washing, caring, and organising to keep the good ship family afloat. You must be a good sailor. I had my daughter in 2009 after only one year of teaching. I hadn't worked long enough to receive maternity leave, so I took six months leave and lived on a government payment for mothers, the baby bonus. I went back part time and visited my husband's shop around the

corner to breast-feed my daughter in the breaks. After three years of part-time, I went back to full time. It's a tough balance—being a mother and a teacher. You never feel like you are doing the best job of either. In the afternoons after school, my daughter waited patiently behind my desk for me to finish. As a result, she has never wanted to be a teacher.

ele

Do we choose a home, or does it choose us?

These are the ties that bind me. It is only here, finding myself in the far north, where I really found myself—and really grew. I headed north an adolescent adult with faith in myself and my future, trust in others and hope in my heart for a fresh start; with eyes and heart open to new experience, ready to work and grow. It wasn't just finding love and having a child, it was about letting go of expectations about what I should be and just doing what I could for others; in my case, young people, who also need to have faith and trust in their elders and the future.

ele

Suddenly one day you catch a glimpse of yourself in a mirror and realise you're looking older. But … you don't mind so much. The lines are mostly laugh lines and show hard-won experience. Without realising, you have shucked off the callow youth, that seeker of vain enjoyment and distraction in all the wrong places—to become quite something else.

ele

Is it that there are fewer cars? Is it that the stars are brighter? Less pollution? Fewer people? That people are kinder? More considerate? Is it being known? Or feeling like you have the space to breathe? Having the whole beach to yourself? That when you see a student down the street, even if they've given you hell in school, they will happily say, "G'day Miss!"? It's all those things, but not just those things.

I decided to end our chat with a little anecdote. Last week at the last minute my husband and I decided to go for a drive to Babinda Boulders. We dove into the crisp, emerald-clear creek and scrambled up on one of the huge boulders that give the creek its name. We had a view of the creek's progress coming and going. I marvelled how the rocks at the water's edge look as if God's hand had laid them out perfectly to enclose the pool. The sun set golden over the tall, wild green tendrils of rainforest. I took a deep breath, inhaling the unspoiled beauty we have to ourselves. I am so glad to be home.

Monsoon Coast

By Laurie Ross Trott

Dorothea loved her sunburnt country
   sowed seeds of childhood awe
   and respect for this wide brown land
   that thrilled her to her core.

   But frequent natural calamities
   have instilled a sense of dread
   of flood and fire and cyclones
   and a fear of what's ahead.

ele

   Frogs chorus from their tea tree swamp
   Pulsing crescendo omph, omph, omph
   bringing in the monsoon rain
   singing wet season round again.

   Tropic summer answers green
   shoots and flush leaf tips are seen
   vibrant vegetation tricks
   hide violent cyclone savaged sticks.

   It's many years past that Yasi came

tearing winds scorched like a flame
casting misery upon the land
lashing all with random hand.

Fluffy toothpicks, the trees appeared
leaves grew on trunks, limbs all sheared
broken, jumbled jungle mess
heaping sadness upon distress.

Cassowaries silent begged for fare
Eden's larder was stripped bare
chopped fruit was cast in dark of night,
for big birds' hungry morning respite.

Useless fit of angered grief
impotent as the fallen leaf
screamed upon a screaming gale
mocking, mocking our travail.

Broken houses, broken trust
paradise lost with every gust
leaving town became the aim
of those who couldn't start again.

Others reached out in their need
and felt the new community seed
feeling stronger yet by far
though each one wore a big wind scar.

Slowly, slowly lives rebuild
threads connect, psyches refill
with taste for life and good times yet
new friends, good fare, and the wild fruit sets.

Frogs' vibrato monsoon song
reminds us where we do belong

it's wild and wet, the tempest coast
green and great, Gondwanan host.

How Could I Ever Leave

By Bruce G Lowe

I sit at my desk, with the sun's first rays filtering golden through the rainforest trees. I'm gazing out at a Kookaburra slapping its beak against the swimming pool fence. Undoubtedly trying to subdue some unfortunate grasshopper or other insect. Will he go for a morning swim after his breakfast? Or will he just fly back up to his favourite branch in the Milky Pine with his three mates who are laughing raucously, seemingly at his expense? He will swim, I bet myself, and not just once but a few times. I win my wager. With one cautious eye watching me sitting at my desk just 10 metres away, he plunges into the clear cool water of the pool like an arrow before erupting skywards in an explosion of spray and feathers. He comes to rest on the pools edge. A whispered Haa ... ha ... haa ... ha breaks the morning silence, not a full-throated Kookaburra laugh, but more a clearing of the lungs, an almost 'Kooka' giggle, a self-satisfied 'damn that felt good kind of noise'.

Two effortless flaps of silver-grey wings and atop the fence he sits again. No time for dallying, he tucks his frame into a projectile once more, and hits the water with all the grace of an Olympic high diver. I wonder who enjoys 'his' morning swims more, him or me? There is something cathartic about watching a wild creature utilise an amenity, which was installed for the human inhabitants of this place. While I ponder this all-important question, a number of other residents wander by scanning me, assessing my threat to them, and probably thinking, 'Hmmph, he's still here'. A Scrub Turkey with his bright red necklace, the ever-present Curlews, a pair of small, heavy-set Wallabies. A large Major Skink, who walks along the pool deck, pauses, looks me up and down with derision, and then slowly ambles off into the shadows away from the days impending heat.

This 'particular' spot in paradise has been my home for a few short years, however, it is very close to Innisfail where I was born. I still live where I was raised, the Cassowary Coast Region, a place of 'truly' outstanding beauty, of majestic waterfalls, streams, and swimming holes, of sun-drenched beaches, unrivalled monsoon rainforests, countless species of animals, birds, plants, and insects, (I'm not kidding, butterflies almost as big as your head), stunning coral reefs and local people, who for the most part are kind, honest and community minded. You know—the kind that would give you the shirt off their back if you needed it more than they did. Sooooo, 'How could I ever leave'?

Leaving this place seemed to be the thing to do for many of the friends I grew up with. Like them, I also went along with the premise, that as soon as we were old enough, we would fly away from here just as fast as we could. Away from the small-town mindset, the multi-generational grouping of families who had been born here, lived all their lives here, and yes, shuffled off their mortal coil here. It amazed me as a young person to learn that there were people who had never strayed more than a few kilometres from the place they were born. That's not for me I'd thought, I'm going to see the world, and never return to this backwater of a place.

Travelling to far off places and witnessing firsthand more of the world's cultures, architecture, and wildlife, became an obsession. Making friends in localities I had never heard of as a child, brought such joy to my small-town soul. Realising there were such staggeringly beautiful destinations to explore, endless new experiences, excitements, and dangers, fuelled my passion for living a most wonderful life away from where I began my journey. Yet as I travelled, I noticed an almost disturbing subliminal trend.

In each of the locations around the globe that I absorbed in my indefatigable attempt to escape my beginnings, I barely noticed that a little voice in my head was comparing the wonderous images of this bright sparkly new world with everything from my home. In many cases, the little voice had found the 'new' not nearly so wonderful as the surroundings I had flourished in as a child.

I first took notice of this voice in 2012 in Brazil. I had travelled to Rio de Janeiro to attend a conference of the International Palm Society. Yes! There is an International Palm Society. There are more than 2600 species of palms, with more being discovered every year. I had begun a love affair with palms in 1981 when I was 16 years of age and had admired the beauty of several impressive palms that were growing in Anzac Square in Brisbane. They were labelled as, *Butia capitata* palms, and grown, I learned, from seeds collected by Australian soldiers while serving overseas during war. I collected some seeds from 'these' palms myself and tried 'unsuccessfully' to grow them. I promptly forgot about palms for quite a few years after that, although the image of their recurved, blue-grey leaves surfaced in my thoughts from time to time.

The 'voice' which had encroached on my thoughts in Brazil, whispered discreetly to me as I enjoyed an enlightening tour of the rainforest near Rio de Janeiro, "the rainforest at home is every bit as good as this ". 'It' was right, the rainforests of North Queensland were indeed every bit as spectacular as those of Brazil, right down to the leeches that had some of our American friends in hysterics. The voice was subtle, discrete, but undeniably present, I quickly dismissed it and enjoyed my wonder filled experiences in Rio and other locations in South America.

I lean back in my chair wondering. In the years following my first encounter with those palms, why I had been in Anzac Square? I guess deep down, I knew what had drawn me inexorably to that place if not the palms. You see, my father, John, had been an Army Major. I had grown up with all thing's 'military' as a young child, not in the way you might think however; there was no dawn bugle, no strict discipline, no marching up and down, indeed, the corners of my mouth have now crept into a smile as I think, ... my father was then, and is still as I write this, a wonderfully caring, loving man. A man whose friends and peers alike, refer to as a 'gentleman', a man of honour, of quiet humility and grace and yet with a kind of strength that has always set him beyond other men, a leader to be admired and looked up to.

I guess I noticed that my father was in uniform from time to time when very young, and Anzac Day marches were always a time to go to the parade and watch my father march with great pride and comradeship. Anzac Day had always been part of my growing up, and so when I visited a new town as I got older, I would seek out places of remembrance. Hence, my visit to Anzac Park in Brisbane at the age of 16. The history, the sacrifice, the mateship, the bloody horrors of war I learnt about, both from my family, from other ex-serviceman and organisations like the RSL, were central in my upbringing. Indeed, as I grew up, I listened intently to ex-servicemen and the stories of their ordeals during conflicts. World War I and II veterans, Korea, Vietnam, and those from other theatres of war. Their stories were horrifically vivid for a teenager, but at times humorous and heart-warming as well, lifechanging for them in almost every instance. It was a sobering thought that at 16, I was the same age as some of them when they went to war. Some of them had come from other countries after the various wars, to work or visit or to pursue a war romance. The one thing they all shared was, 'they never left'. One old English soldier once told me, "I came here for one job! When I left England, I was laying bricks on a job site and the water in my bucket froze, I took a job offer here and never left; better to melt in the North Queensland summer than freeze to death".

— *ele* —

Crash! A bedraggled kookaburra sits stunned on the deck outside the sliding glass doors. He taps at the glass, his beak gleaming, black, and smooth, an almost disdainful expression in his shining eyes. Tilting his head, he looks up at me, taps the glass twice more, and flies back to the pool fence, apparently none the worse for the collision. "You have got to stop doing that! Seriously, you are going to do yourself an injury you stupid bird." My words seem to draw a response this time; he cocks his head and begins to laugh. His mates up in the Milky Pine join him in a chorus, and oh, what a glorious sound it is in the stillness of the early morning. In some legends of our First Nations People, the raucous laughter of the Kookaburra is a signal to the Sky People to start the day by lighting the great fire that warms the Earth.

I am uncertain of my feathered friend's thought processes when it comes to flying into the glass doors after he swims some days. It has become a semi regular thing, so much so that there are several, large, bird shaped smudges on the glass from his more recent assaults on the doors. Perhaps he sees a rival in his own image reflected back at him. As the exuberance of their laughter dwindles, my wet friend flies high into the trees, joining his flock, refreshed from his swim and perhaps prepared for his day. I am glad his aerobatic antics seem to leave him unscathed; I don't think 'I' would fair so well if I hit that glass with such force, I'm certain it would leave 'me' damaged.

My beautiful wife is an incredible artist and author. She has written, illustrated and published books in multiple genres and her fine art adorns walls and galleries all over the world. She is an optimist, a believer in unicorns and fairies, and is also of the opinion that I have damaged myself quite a lot in my life. I have, I feel, been incredibly lucky when it comes to injuries, considering all the amazing experiences I have had in my younger years. I have trekked through untouched rainforests, climbed some of Queensland's highest mountains, hell! I've ridden trail bikes up mountains. Swum in every creek, river, mountain stream and ocean I could. Jumping off some waterfalls, sliding down others, fishing, camping, being chased by feral pigs, chased by a cassowary, being stung by five different kinds of jellyfish, (two of the deadly ones) coming face to face with a shark, seeing crocodiles up close in the wild, even having had one follow the very small boat I was rowing, catching snakes, sinking boats, rolling cars, blowing things up, and that was all before I was twenty years of age.

These scary, exciting, and at times stupid exploits, were, I realise, only a miniscule fraction of my life. Diluted by a stable loving family, the relative safety of living in a small community and much later in life, and an epiphany of just how incredible my surroundings are, both when I was a child and to the current day. It was just how my life growing up was, I guess, so I did not think it was anything special. Walking through tunnel like, rainforest tracks with my grandparents (all four of them at times) having them show me birds and animals; my brothers and cousins encouraged, just for fun, to chase after the spectacular 'blue mountain' (Ulysses) butterflies. Emerging from the jungle onto stunning beaches like Ella Bay. Spending the hot north Queensland summers swimming, playing in the trees, making little pools in the sand to observe the tiny fish, crabs, starfish, and any other creatures we could catch. Thousands of experiences like these; far, far too many life-changing moments to transcribe onto these pages were filed away in my brain and created the little 'travel' voice in my head. Travelling, I reminisce, was something that I began doing fairly early in life. My parents and grandparents instilled in me their great love of travel. In 1976 our grandparents took my 11-year-old self and my older brother and our cousin to the United States of America. This was a different time in the world, a time of prosperity for many countries, and the USA was a bright shining beacon of affluence. Disneyland, the Grand Canyon, Knott's Berry Farm, Holiday Inn, Universal Studios, to name but a few icons of Bicentennial US society we experienced. Again, there it is, 45 years later. I remember in all the childhood exuberance of that trip, a little voice whispered to me that our beaches were nicer than the famous Waikiki in Hawaii as I stumbled over coral ledges in that blue green surf.

Contented in the serenity of my thoughts as I write, I stretch my legs out into the warming autumn sunshine now falling upon the tiles, having crept its way above the trees nearest the house. Rainforest covered banks slope steeply away to my right some sixty metres, greeting the ever-present cascading of clear, lifegiving mountain water, flowing over moss covered stones worn smooth by eons of monsoon rains. Epiphytic vines cling to ancient trees, dangling their leaf tips in the stream as it feeds the forest's inhabitants. Tree ferns and their cousins the King ferns reach from the water's edge with their immense nine-metre-long fronds into filtered sunlight, just as they have done for some two hundred and fifty million years. Oh . . . and palms . . . yes! There are at least ten species of palms that are native to my home, who would have thought? Perhaps it's time to make myself another coffee.

ele

Thinking of coffee, I recall a trip to Vanuatu in Fiji. An ocean cruise this time. I befriended a porter who worked on the cruise ship; it was his day off when we reached Vanuatu and he offered to show me around, having been there many times with his work. He was Italian and we had to have a coffee before we left the wharf, he said. There was a makeshift coffee stall and the owner knew my new friend very well. Without being asked he gave us a very small cup each; coffee you could almost stand a spoon up in, it was that thick, just as my Italian friend liked it. Sightseeing on Vanuatu was spectacular; diving on the coral reefs and old shipwrecks was an amazing experience. But there it was once more, the murmuring in my head, that home had reefs and wrecks and nature that was equal, if not better. Similar thoughts dogged me on a dozen Fijian islands after that.

Turning my chair away from the desk to go and boil the kettle, a small, brilliantly coloured money spider decides to join me for a walk to the kitchen. Leaping from the screen of my laptop, he lands on my forearm and wanders down to my hand. I try to baffle him by moving my fingers up and down as I stroll to the kitchen. He manoeuvres from finger to finger with ease and waggles his palps at me as if to say "is that all you've got". "I think you should be out on one of my plants," I tell him, and deposit him on a rare Madagascan palm I have growing in a pot near the kitchen door.

The nearest I ever got to Madagascar, which is the home of many of the world's rarest palm species, was when I visited the island of Mauritius in 2017. It also has palms, some of the most endangered on the planet. Mauritius was the home of the extinct Dodo bird and is a ruggedly beautiful place, born of more than twenty volcanoes. Originally uninhabited, it was colonised by the Dutch in 1598 but was later abandoned. The French took control in 1715 and then Great Britain seized it in 1810. Mauritius gained independence in 1968. Once again, my whispering companion compared the surroundings, the reefs, the beaches and as usual reminded me that "home" was better. However, it is noteworthy that nowhere else have I experienced such multiculturalism as Mauritius, which seems to have achieved what countries like Australia have so desperately strived for. During my short time there I attended gatherings in various settings, including social clubs, restaurants, resorts, and bars frequented by locals. I have never seen such an acceptance of race, culture and religion as I experienced on Mauritius. It is the one place on the planet my traveling voice could not say in that regard at least that "home is better". Fresh coffee in hand, I recall just how deeply it struck me in Mauritius to see so many nationalities and religions blending, accepting one another for who they were as people, not what their backgrounds were.

"Hello" … there is the tiniest of tap–tap–tapping on my finger resting on my desk—the Money Spider is back. He jumps onto my wrist and struggles through the untidy hair on my forearm. Jump, jump, jump, and he's sitting on my shoulder like an eight-legged Jiminy Cricket. "Are you to be my conscience now?" I ask with a laugh. He wiggles his little green and red palps and, despite me wishing he would, he says nothing. "I think we are doing okay though, don't you?" He tilts his tiny head as if listening intently but again says nothing. "North Queensland is perhaps the most multicultural place in Australia, at least I think so, what do you think?" More palp waving. "You don't say much, do you? Let me tell you what I think." With full acceptance of the fact that European settlers wrongfully displaced the Aboriginal peoples of Australia and committed terrible crimes against them, the blended nationalities that now inhabit the north can be truly proud of their ancestries. Including the original inhabitants of this great nation, there are some two hundred and seventy ethnic groups in Australia. For the most part, we all get along pretty well. Distinctive architecture, customs, and religions make up the diverse modern history of the north—Chinese temples, Aboriginal sacred sites, culture and artworks, Italian restaurants and design, art deco buildings, mosques, Seik temples, churches. So, so, many styles, cultures and peoples interwoven, very close to my home, even a Spanish castle, called Paronella Park. Growing up in this place, you fail to notice when you're young just how many different cultures surround you. They are just part of your world, analogous to the way you fail to recognise your amazing surroundings … they intertwine with your very existence because they just 'are'.

With that brilliant piece of deductive reasoning fresh in his little green head, my Money Spider companion moves to my elbow, jumps onto my laptop, and follows a small ant across my desk. Was he just using my shoulder as a vantage point to assess where his next meal was coming from? I wish to believe he concluded that I was correct in my assertions and no longer needed his counsel, so decided to return to his rainforest home.

The rainforest he calls home is among the oldest on the planet. It is estimated that the northern Australian forests are eighty million years older than the Amazon rainforests. They are home to over six hundred and fifty species of animals, reptiles, and birds along with countless species of insects, including two hundred and thirty species of butterflies. Many of the areas close by are included the Queensland Wet Tropics World Heritage Area. Yes, it can be wet—you can't have some of the best rainforest in the World without rain. I have known years where it has rained for more than 300 days; in fact, 2010 had 310 wet days, more if you count the days of drizzle. The number of wet days usually averages about 166 days a year. From time to time we have endured some severe tropical cyclones; I have lived through three direct hits by cyclones in the past 40 years. They can be devastating, both physically to the environment and infrastructure, as well as mentally on those who experience them. Many places on Earth experience various forms of natural disasters. There is nothing humans can do to stop them and so I choose not to live my life being concerned about them.

The creatures that are part of the rainforest ecosystem are wonderous, beautiful, breathtaking, and at times, can be dangerous. The southern Cassowary is visually striking and one of the largest flightless birds on Earth, the region we live in holds their name, The Cassowary Coast. Observed from a distance they are a joy to behold, although like all wild creatures, they should be left alone, or they are more than able to defend themselves. Platypus, echidna, turtles, bandicoots, and many other creatures grace our little patch of paradise, very cute, but still wild creatures. There are also many dangerous creatures in the region, snakes, crocodiles, spiders, jellyfish to name but a few. Except for the occasional python that finds its way into the house, the rest are easily and wisely avoided.

During my travels around the world, residents of various countries have expressed concern at the array of creatures that can "kill you" residing in Australia. I simply reply that we don't have war or famine; where I live there is no overcrowding, no mass shootings, no terrorism, no rampant disease, few muggings, virtually no air pollution, the water is safe to drink and generally life is 'pretty damn good'.

—eee—

A hand now touches my shoulder. Jerking upright, I almost give myself whiplash in fright. "Would you like another coffee?" says the voice attached to the hand. "Holy crap you scared me" is my initial response, followed by "yes please". My wife's two adult sons had warned me that their mother possessed "Ninja like stealth", and she had proved it to me on many occasions since. I sometimes amuse myself considering that believers in unicorns and fairies require this kind of stealth in order to observe them without frightening them away.

My wife and I have both been married once before and we have two, adult children each, three of the four have moved away from here; there are beautiful grandchildren brightening our lives now as well. Having them experience the things I have in my life would be my deepest wish and I think in their hearts they still call this place home. A short time after we met, my wife learnt of my passion for rare palms and on our first Christmas together she gifted me some dirt. More precisely, she made me an offer to plant some of the rare palms that I had collected from around the world on her property, as well a place to erect a new greenhouse to begin collecting more. The greenhouse is now built, it is attached to a guest house nestled in existing gardens my wife lovingly planted with all kinds of plants over the past twenty or so years, restoring to rainforest some of what had been cleared for farming. I have now added my touch to this paradise. Rare and endangered palms and other plants from all over our world now flourish in our tropical oasis. When I mention to people that I grow rare palms, their responses vary from "wow, what kinds", to "there are rare palms"? The reality is that there is such a huge array of different palms from all parts of the world that only a small number are grown commercially for the gardening public. The reasons behind this vary from how easily they grow and how difficult it is to obtain seeds in large quantities to those species where loss of habitat has pushed them to the brink of extinction and they are protected by international laws that prohibit collection.

To understand the diversity of palms could quite literally take a lifetime, but in short, palm species range in size from 200mm (eight inches) tall to 60 metres (200 feet) tall. They hold the record for the largest leaves in nature, held by *Raphia regalis* at 24 metres (80 feet) long and also the largest seed known in nature, *Lodociea maldivica*, weighing in at 20 kilos and a metre in circumference. They have many different leaf shapes, from feather, to fan, to wedge, to paddle shaped and others, the foliage can be spotted, tessellated, striped, mottled, variegated, and coloured. Some palms put on exuberant displays of colour when a new leaf opens. I have seen new leaves show as blood red, maroon, bright pink, black, brown, yellow, purple, orange, and more, some are nothing shy of breathtaking. Some palms even have different coloured trunks and crown shafts, like the commonly sold 'Lipstick' palms with their red trunks. Other rare palms have pink, orange, maroon, purple, blue (yes blue), white, yellow, black, facets and some are even striped like the skin of a watermelon.

My hope is to preserve, for the generations to come, species that are critically endangered or in some cases, are technically extinct in their native habitats already, an ark of sorts. My links with a community of dedicated plant enthusiasts has ensured many wonderful friendships across the globe and is in many of my recent years, my main reason for traveling. Now my life companion adds her joy of traveling to my own, showing me wonderous destinations where I had never been, while indulging, and I think enjoying, my obsession with palms.

I'm certain my wife and I would love to have a chateau in the south of France or a villa in Spain to spend time away in if we were wealthy. Our shared time in Europe after we married was awe inspiring, at times even overwhelming. I recall vividly standing in the midst of Gaudi's breathtaking cathedral in Barcelona, 'La Sagrada Familia' and weeping with uncontrollable emotion at the resplendent magnificence of this yet to be completed masterpiece. The unrivalled historical architecture and ageless beauty of Europe's most celebrated cultures is so inspiring. However, the ever-present narrator in my head reminded me amidst all the beauty that I have always felt the cold, and for me, a lad from the tropics, anything below 18 degrees Celsius is cold and Europe gets bloody cold. Then there are the machine-gun wielding police and military in most of Europe's cities, most of South America and North America, and violent demonstrations in several cities I've visited, which make for an uneasy reminder of insecurities we do not face at home.

Not since the early 1930's during the days of the infamous 'Black Hand Gang' has there been any persistent crime in the region, certainly nothing like the problems experienced in the larger cities of the world. My grandfather on my father's side, moved to this area in 1928, and worked hard his entire life to help secure a good life for his family. He travelled extensively around the world, moved around the north in later years, but always returned home. He would joke about the rain, often saying "any man who would predict the weather in Innisfail more than five minutes in advance, was touched in the head". His many enthralling stories of both unimaginable hardships faced in the early 1900's and years of affluence and prosperity in the early days of the north, made it clear that he loved this place he had chosen to call home. Frank Lowe was a strong, no-nonsense type of man, but I saw in his eyes a softness. When my grandmother died suddenly, his grief consumed him for a time, but eventually he got on with life and travelled a little more, even into his eighties. His heart, however, was forever broken at the loss of his Ruby, my grandmother. Before he passed away some twenty years later at 92, he told me of missing her every single day. I regret I was minutes too late to arrive at the hospital the night he died. I sat and talked to him even though he was gone. I held his giant, once calloused hands that were now soft as silk. His work was done. I whispered "goodbye old man" kissed his forehead and left him at peace, in the knowledge that he was home.

Another splash, I raise my head to see smooth circular ripples spreading across the surface of the pool once more, the sound, in unison with a reminiscent tear falling onto my keyboard. The brilliantly coloured Azure Kingfisher is much smaller than its Kookaburra cousins but enjoys a swim just as much it would seem. Exuberant shades of turquoise blue feathers, softened by sunset orange, black and white, bring happiness back into my morning. There is no vociferous laughter like his cousins, just a quiet almost smiling confidence as he sits flicking the pool water from his wings with his shining, midnight black beak. Turning his head, a split-second fluttering, on the wing he snatches a small fish from my nearby pond and vanishes into the emerald green of the rainforest. "Dammit, another fish gone", I mutter. Contempt shown by the local wildlife to most things humans try to add or change in a landscape is universal. An affront to Mother Nature it seems, and therefore, it becomes a challenge for them to see if they can correct things. In reality, they are just doing what wild creatures do. I really need to not take to heart, the disappearance of a few fish or my rare palms being dug up by Scrub Hens or eaten by native rats and wallabies, they don't do it out of any malice, I'm sure. Or do they? I chuckle to myself. Many times, I have had native White Tail Rats walk right past a common plant, only to eat something incredibly rare from Madagascar, Sarawak, or Costa Rica. Perhaps they just have expensive, exotic tastes in plants.

Growing rare Palms is challenging for many of my friends worldwide. Weather, animals, insects, and plant diseases are something growers of exotic plants have to accept with grace, although a few of my American friends who deal with gophers eating and killing some of their very rare species, struggle to retain much composure at. "You see", my travel voice says, "there is always someone having to deal with more challenging creatures than you have to". So now my collection of rare palms continues to expand. Beautiful plants from all over the globe flourish amongst the rainforest, in a climate perfectly adapted for growing almost anything. My Mother, rest her soul, used to say if you stand still long enough in North Queensland, you will either take root, or something else will begin to grow on you. Elwyn was her name, my father's greatest support and lifelong love. A strong, intelligent, loving person, whose family meant everything to her, she was fiercely loyal to family and friends alike. My brothers and I could not have wished for a better mother although, like most children, we perhaps did not appreciate her as much as we should have. A bleed on the brain while traveling in Europe was to eventually take her from us but not before we got to spend a little more time with her. There were very lucid moments in an Austrian hospital where she recognised my father, brother and I at her bedside and flashes of memories of her childhood growing up in the north. Like most of my family, my mother loved to travel, and it is comforting that some of her last memories were of travelling and thoughts of home, which is where she was always happiest.

Happiness, it's said, is one of life's greatest rewards. Innumerable people around the world are born into abject poverty, incredibly harsh surroundings, wars, famine, crime and violence, from which they never manage to escape. I have seen only the very edges of such lives in my travels, skated luckily along the periphery of the horrors that some people face in their day-to-day existence. I have also seen some of the world's greatest wonders, become friends with some extraordinary people from over 30 different countries I've visited, while drinking in their cultures, scenery, and hospitality, like a man drinks water if dying of thirst.

My 'travel voice' will always be with me but it won't stop me from wanting to travel. It is my constant reminder, a remembrance that I come from one of the most beautiful places on our planet, a place of peace and prosperity. My life is filled with the love of an amazing woman, of my beautiful children, two wonderfully welcoming stepsons, grandchildren, other family members and friends. I also now get to watch some of the rarest palms on Earth grow to maturity after nurturing them in pots, in some cases for many years. I hope that friends and visitors from all over the world will be able to come and stay and admire what I am so lucky to have been blessed with. They will marvel at their surroundings and comment how stunning it really is, to which I will reply, "that's why I stayed".

Windows

By Barbara Bufi

My old house sits on a hill,
   faced west towards high mountains,
   tried by cyclone many times.
I rejoice in its windows,
   kept wide open to the world
   to bring in the cooling breeze.

Through these oblong openings
wonders enter every day
to enrich my living space.
Bartle Frere, head wreathed in cloud,
greets me in the predawn hush
as sunlight gilds its summit.

North windows in December
show bright lights twinkling nightly
on the Tower Christmas tree;
red berries, golden blossom,
decorate green-strapped palm fronds
Christmas dress for the tropics.

Eastward, morning colours glow,
bathing grass where white ibis
probe for food with billhook beaks;
day's end from my veranda,

sunset's red gold evening kiss
paints the western windows pink.

At night a tropical moon
lends silver incandescence,
gleaming softly off the glass;
as I sleep the Southern Cross,
low in the star spangled sky
shines blessings through my windows.

My old house sits on the hill,
walls imbued with memories
its windows framing wonders;
love and marriage called me here,
ties of love and family bind me,
because of these I have stayed.

Black Ribbon

By Jacque Duffy

"Broken Nose. I think you'll find it's called Broken Nose." I was stunned. How could something so incredibly magnificent have a name that belonged to a boxer's face? Although now I think about it, the profound effect seeing it had on me was akin to a punch to the face so, perhaps, the name is appropriate. I had journeyed to the Far North to visit a friend. She worked as a journalist and to my surprise had landed a job at the Cairns Post. I wasn't surprised she had the job, don't get me wrong, she's an amazing writer and editor. My surprise came from my reliable and organised friend not coming home to Brisbane . . . she was on holiday as far as I was concerned. She and her partner had gone on a road trip together, camping in national parks. Apparently, they got as far as Cairns and decided they couldn't leave. It was too beautiful. They aren't the only ones to do this; it's something many people do when they visit the tropics.

I can understand why they stay. There is a special magic about the north. It wrapped its sticky tendrils of spells around me too. I experienced what I can only describe as a 'spiritual moment' when I first laid eyes on Broken Nose. As you travel north up the Bruce Highway about ten minutes out of Innisfail, after you've just driven through an area of gentle rolling hills, sugarcane, and cattle pastures, you're delivered to a cutting with fern covered walls. The cutting wends its way to higher ground. Then suddenly, for mere seconds, as your speeding vehicle clears the crest, you're faced with an enormous open space, and in the near distance, a glimpse of Queensland's highest mountain, Bartle Frere. What you see–on a clear day–is the southern end, a jagged beak that points toward Ravenshoe, its mass protruding high up but only some way toward the invisible peak. Broken Nose. For sheer seconds you take in the majesty of it as it steals your breath. Then you roller coaster down the black ribbon to be plunged into a tunnel of new growth rainforest before being spat out at the feet of the giant mountain. You can almost hear it whisper, "I am the matriarch. Welcome to my embrace".

At the very moment my car crested that hill, I had an overwhelming feeling that I had been here before. A feeling that I belonged, and this was my home. Except, I had never been here before. It was such a powerful feeling, emotional yes, but strangely physical too, I actually felt nauseous. I tried to explain this experience to my friend. I'm not sure she understood, I'm not even sure I understand myself. Maybe it was just the awesomeness of the mountain after so many rolling green hills. Maybe I got a fright as the car crested the hill and I wasn't prepared for the open space . . . I don't know. What I do know is, I decided in that very moment, somehow I was going to make this place my own. I crested that rise quite a few more times in the following years before I planted my feet here. Each time the mountain spoke to me, and still does, nearly thirty years later.

I have often thought about the intense way I was drawn to this place. Magnetic. Unmistakably irresistible. Almost hypnotic in the way I was spoken to by an invisible presence, a voice inside me. Was it my soul? No. I don't think so. But I must admit there is a certain supernatural quality about this area in the north. It manages to draw interesting and creative people to it. I have noticed numerous artists live in this area. Most have come from somewhere else to make their creative space in the shadow of the mountain.

As an artist and writer, I guess I notice things other people may not; perhaps what I see is reliant on my vivid imagination. Perhaps they notice them too but have a different name for them. This place is a place of contrast and juxtaposition.

Beneath Broken Nose is one of the accessible entrances to Wooroonooran National Park, part of the Wet Tropics World Heritage Area. It is home to some of the oldest surviving rainforest on the planet. The ease of access versus the impenetrable wall of rainforest that greets you is just one of my favourite contrasts. Be brave, be determined. You will discover the pathways; they are what appear to be small dark holes in the vegetation and resemble dark tunnels that lead deep into the forest. Please note the signage as you pass, stinging plants are real, and you do not want to meet one. If you do, you will be taking home a souvenir of pain that will last a lifetime–enjoy.

Step inside the dark tunnel and walk a few metres. Stop. Listen. Stand still a moment. The dark tunnel has transformed into light filled space. Do you feel insignificant standing here inside Nature's Cathedral? Do you feel you are being watched? You are. Look up. The absolute ceiling of this cathedral is impossible to see. Between the undersides of dark leaves sunlight pushes its way through. Blinding. Like an enormous room with mirror balls, spears of light dart, kaleidoscope like, in various directions spotlighting artworks of nature. As you walk the pathways that weave their way between the buttress roots of tall trees take note of the delicate ferns and fungi that cling to impossible surfaces. Witness how the colours change on tree trunks. Can you hear the trickle of running water? Walking through the forest is like walking through a city of solid, tall buildings, around every turn there is something undiscovered, waiting for you. A creek crosses your path, so does a tiny turtle. Thirsty? Take a drink. This is the cleanest, freshest water you have ever tasted . . . unless you've been here before.

Inside the rainforest you can be hot and cool at the same time. It has its own climate. A natural humidicrib. Moisture beads on your face, if you look closely, you will notice that many leaves also have perspiration on them. As though a giant has mis-stepped and left a devastating footprint, you've come across a large sunny area of broken growth. The scar looks permanent. Except saplings are bravely pushing their way toward the sky, manoeuvring between the detritus of smashed timber and tangled vines which wrap around an enormous ancient-looking, fallen tree trunk. I imagine this giant of a tree falling, taking with it a chunk of forest. I wonder, did anyone hear it fall?

A flash of luminous blue catches your eye. Ulysses and Cairns Birdwing butterflies decorate the forest with games of hide and seek. As they flutter, stand still and you might get lucky. If you're wearing something colourful one may land on you; if it does, you've been brushed with magic. There is blue underfoot too, winter and spring, local Quandong trees feed the forest animals and birds.

When you hear something that sounds like the static of an old television set, you know you are getting closer; you've almost reached the jewel in this part of the national park. Josephine Falls. The wall of trees opens onto Josephine Creek. As though you've just removed earmuffs, you are deafened by the roar of water . . . step back a few paces into the forest and noise mellows . . . step out again and witness the power of white water pounding smoothed boulders. Standing at the lowest lookout and absorbing three levels of Josephine Falls in all its grandeur is breathtaking. Beautiful just doesn't describe it. The pummelling of the water is so powerful it can be felt in your chest when you stand in such close proximity. It creates its own breeze. The rockslide and bottom pool on a sunny day will be full of locals and tourists. It's great fun skiing down the slippery rockface before splashing into the freezing water. Delicate Ulysses fluttering among people, boulders, and giant trees, and then casually dipping and gliding near the raging water is one juxtaposition that never fails to impress upon me just how amazing this part of the world is.

As an artist I am often stopped in my tracks and can't proceed on my journey without acknowledging the enormity of effect something has on me. I see colours, design, contrast, and symmetry everywhere. Broken Nose and Josephine Falls have captured me. I have never drawn or painted these places. I honestly have no desire to try to recreate something so impressive. I don't believe I could capture the essence, nor the immensity of presence. But it isn't about being big, or enormous. Josephine Falls, although a magnificent spectacle, is also a myriad of tiny things that are worth paying attention to: The shape of a fallen leaf, moss covering a stone, a fungus with delicate and intricate edging. This is a place to slow yourself, a place to slow the way you look and think about things, a place to slow your breathing and slow your busy mind.

―――ℓℓ――

Driving the black ribbon that wraps itself around the rolling hills of the Cassowary Coast is an experience that differs from day to day, hour to hour. A shower of rain here is classified as a downpour in other parts of Australia. Our rain showers have clean edges—it can be heavy, fat raindrops on one side of a house and clear on the other. You can hear the rain coming as it pummels the trees; I have at times mistaken it for a truck travelling along the road. On a hot day, with the sun trying to beat you into submission, it can rain. A fine mist that glistens in the sunshine. The humid air has liquefied, like it simply overextended itself. When this happens, driving becomes challenging, as the now wet black ribbon becomes a shattered mirror, reflecting sunshine directly into unsuspecting eyes. Beauty sometimes comes with unwelcome side effects.

The Cassowary Coast is in the Wet Tropics and it is the land of rainbows. It is not unusual to see a double rainbow or to see three rainbows in one area. I have found it almost impossible to catch this phenomenon with a camera because these rainbows are fluid creatures moving about with minds of their own. I often imagine an Australian version of the Leprechaun running wildly around searching for his pots of gold. As you drive around the Cassowary Coast, you catch glimpses of Bartle Frere and Broken

Nose. Occasionally, especially in cane harvesting season, you're treated to an open vista with the mountain proudly taking centre stage. Daily, locals are fortunate enough to witness the setting sun drape the mountain in its ever-changing cape of luminosity.

Our black ribbon that caresses the verdant hills also leads to nearby hidden beaches. These beaches are kissed by more than sunshine and the sparkling waters of the Coral Sea. The rainforest lovingly reaches out and runs its fingers in the coarse sand. Cassowaries leave their footprints beside that of human visitors. We co-exist, but the cassowary is to be respected. They are experts in the game of hide and seek. In and out of the shadows on beaches and the edges of rainforest. Don't feed these ancient birds to encourage them closer. They can be dangerous and although they grace us with their presence they are wild creatures and remain untamed. They are free and protected. Please be cautious when traversing the black ribbons to the beaches, cassowaries don't have road sense.

This is a place of exotic creatures and immense beauty. A place of contradictions too. It is hot, cold, hard and soft, nurturing and dangerous. I have lived here for more than half my lifetime now. The friend I came to visit all those years ago is still in the north too. Her north is different from mine. She has chosen Palm Cove as her home. Her north has a beauty of its own. I had considered moving closer to her, but this place and its magic has captured me.

As Good as it Gets

By Laurie Ross Trott

Leaving was never an option. First, there's the dilemma of where to go. Move to the city to be closer to the kids? No, not because I wouldn't like to see more of them but the idea of the boring isolation and anonymity of rampant suburbia holds, for me, a terror all of its own. And then there is the reality of being older and all that that entails, from my perspective and the attitude of some towards older people—to be patronised or worse, to be invisible and ignored. I love the trappings of city life such as the theatre and art galleries, travelling shows and the diverse choice of eateries reflecting Australia's multicultural community. But give me village life any day, where it is just the right size—small enough to recognise and acknowledge others and to enjoy the same life-affirming response yourself, and big enough for everyone to mind their own business.

Two top of the scale cyclones in five years is a pretty rough deal but many of those who fled the cyclone-prone tropics and headed south have found that climate change has followed them. Every year huge storms in the south uproot trees and lift the roofs from houses. Hail storms batter cars and crops and cause big dollar damage. This year places further south have also endured tragic and devastating floods with repeated rain systems blowing in from the ocean. Our summer storms are usually not violent and the downpours heavy and brief. The air is alive with a quickening of thunder and lightning. Our amphibian friends add to the tropical atmosphere, stirred to begin their mating calls, which will build to a full-on frog chorus when the wet season proper gets under way. Our annual rainfall average is about three-and-a-half metres and the warm rain can beat a steady tattoo on the roof for days at a time.

We were hydroponic lettuce and herb farmers of only a few months when cyclone Larry smashed into the Cassowary Coast. We had made the 'green change' from our journalist jobs in another state to return to my native Far North Queensland and our favourite holiday destination of Mission Beach. While farming was in the blood, we were finding water-based, table-top horticulture a steep learning curve. There was no expert advice on 'legal' hydroponic crops to be had locally; any agronomy advice was tailored towards bananas and sugar cane, the big crops in this region. We were grateful to find a book online on hydroponic farming in the much cooler climate of New Zealand. Lesson number one: farm for local conditions. Despite not having a veggie oracle to advise us on why our cool climate vegetables were failing to thrive in the steamy tropics regardless of our best efforts, we finally worked out why. Our frustrating puzzler of a problem was root rot caused by the high summer temperature and spread by the recirculating nutrient flow. We had no option but to mulch thousands of struggling plants, scrub and bleach the food-grade plastic growing channels, empty and sanitize our four-thousand-litre tank and start again. We were rewarded with a beautiful crop and our return to trading and first harvest was scheduled for March 20, 2006 ...

That was the day of cyclone Larry, a menacing twister of destructive energy that started as a tropical depression in the Coral Sea and built to a category five fury, the highest on the scale. Day after day, we plotted its progress on the cyclone chart as it moved relentlessly westward towards Innisfail, our regional centre just north of Mission Beach. It dropped to a category four after crossing the coast but caused an estimated half a billion dollars in damage to infrastructure and crops. It flattened or damaged around 10,000 homes. The government scientific body

CSIRO clocked an Australian record wind gust of 293.7kph on the eastern slopes of nearby Mt Bartle Frere.

It had been 20 years since Winifred, the previous big cyclone, had thrashed the region, and I guess we were complacent. We were a little bemused the day before Larry crossed the coast when we arrived at the annual Feast of the Senses, a foodie fiesta of ultra-tropical fruit and all things local food-wise, in Innisfail to find officials moving among the thinning crowd exclaiming through loud hailers, "go home, go home, there is a cyclone coming". So we went home, rolled up and stowed hoses and other loose items, moved inside from the verandahs the boxes of household stuff and keepsakes we'd packed months previously in Perth and had had no time to attend to, and gathered up the shed cat who came with the farm. And waited. During the night the power went out and stayed out for nearly three weeks. At 6am the rain was horizontal and we sheltered in the bathroom, the second smallest room in the house, with the cat, unused to such niceties, curled up in the makeshift litter box filled with water filtration medium. We perched on the side of the bathtub wearing our bicycle helmets and head torches and felt as foolish as the flashlight reflection in the large bathroom mirror told us we looked. But the noise, like screaming jet engines with a wobble in the roar, was terrifying. I called a sister. "Pray for us". My religiously inclined siblings still like to recount that story.

In the dim, early light, I watched as the furious winds tore loose the plastic rain covers from our hydroponics greenhouses, which then wrapped around the steel support hoops, wrenching them free and turning them into agents of destruction, like threshing machines wielded by a demonic, invisible hand.

When it was safe to venture from the house we walked amidst what seemed like surreal scenes. Humility lodged in our chests, an unspeakable tightness that escaped as a murmured, "wow" or "oh my God, look at that". We were truly awed by nature's might, realising how incidental and powerless we are in the face of such a brutal phenomenon. Our 250 metres of four-metre-high greenhouses were twisted wrecks and many of our hydro tables were damaged and smashed by the flailing steel hoops. Astonishingly, some of the smaller, younger lettuces still occupied their holes in the hydro channels but a thousand or so had been shanghaied by the wind. I later wrote:

There's more to lettuce than you think
'cos' lettuces can fly
I learnt that when Larry came
and blew them all sky high!

The World Heritage listed rainforest across the road was unrecognisable; wind-burnt, splintered and broken trees stripped of their leaves stood stark and bare, revealing the contours of the hills and ridges once hidden by lush greenery. On our side of the El Arish – Mission Beach Road, beautiful rainforest giants were toppled, along with enormous ornamental Cuban Royals and other exotic and native palms. Our farmhouse, graffitied from roof to verandah floor with shredded-leaf confetti, had withstood the onslaught though the horizontal rain had found a way in between the closed glass louvres tucked beneath the shelter of four-metre-wide verandahs. Without a cohort of close friends in our new home town and with few family members around at that time, we were overwhelmed, feeling stressed and alone in a broken world. We worked hard by day clearing up the mess and when daylight ran out our neighbours joined us on our back verandah for mosquito coil scented, candlelit dinners. For a few nights we enjoyed feasts, including our take on Beef Wellington cooked on the gas barbecue, and other fare from the freezer, consuming what we could before it spoiled. We gathered up fallen mangosteens from our thrashed crop and discovered the 'Queen of Tropical Fruit' adds a delicious lift to champagne. We loaned a friend of our neighbours a spare generator and she, a cook, sent back tasty pizzas. We needed to work and in order to do so needed to play, making truth of the saying, 'If you don't laugh, you'll cry'. This brief window of frivolity staved off the blues waiting to crowd us with more darkness in our traumatised world.

The task of cleaning up was enormous. Telephone connection was out, and we had no mains power for 19 days, though power companies from around the nation sent emergency crews to help get life back to 'normal'. The army, Red Cross and other organisations and volunteer groups provided much appreciated help throughout the region. We were grateful to 'Blaze Aid' volunteers who did their best to sort the twisted mess of posts, wires and vines that had been our two-acre (almost a hectare) passionfruit orchard. Thankfully, the government provided financial assistance to get rural industries and businesses back into operation and to restore productivity as quickly as possible.

Life eventually returned to 'normal' and we were no longer so complacent about the fury of a tropical cyclone. Some people packed up and left. Others were more pragmatic, reflecting that the previous big 'blow' had been two decades earlier. …

But five years later it felt like Ground Hog Day. Here we go again! Cyclone Yasi blew in from the warm waters around Fiji, bigger, meaner and off the scale scary. We did not want to be around for her forecast night-time performance, blind to happenings on the other side of the windows and terrified by the screaming wind and the crashing and banging of falling forest friends. We gratefully accepted my sister Leanne's kind invitation to shelter with other family members at her home at Atherton, 130km inland.

We prepared for the 'blow', and once it seemed sure that Yasi was going to hit we made the decision to sacrifice the rain covers on our greenhouses in the hope of saving the steel and timber structures. We worked beyond exhaustion in the steaming February humidity, climbing up and down ladders along our quarter kilometre of greenhouses, cutting free and hauling down the plastic. With aching arms we tugged the sheeting over the ground, folded it up and loaded it into our delivery vehicle to take to the rubbish tip after the cyclone had passed. That was if it was still intact inside the packing shed when we returned. Another of my sisters called a number of times, her growing concern interrupting our efforts to secure as much as we could on the farm. The Queensland Premier had declared a state of emergency and people on the beachfront, nine kilometres from Quandong Farm, had been ordered to evacuate because of fears of a tidal surge.

The phone went again. "You've got to get out now, we're all here at Atherton and they're closing the roads at two o'clock"; then "you can't come, you've got to stay there, it's two o'clock". Finally, some time after two o'clock, we packed up the new cat, a small chainsaw and supplies and literally headed for the hills, knowing Yasi would not make landfall for some hours yet. The drive along the silent highway devoid of people, vehicles and activity was eerie. It was the same on the 'Great Green Way', meandering past quiet farmhouses and empty paddocks, between neat plantations of towering sugar cane and bananas, their leaves tickled by a gentle breeze. We encountered just five vehicles in the hour-and-a-half journey. The lack of people and normal work-a-day activity made it feel like something apocalyptic had already occurred.

Nine family members sheltered at Leanne and Tim's home on the outskirts of Atherton, along with our nephew Nick's Staffy, Diesel, our cat Oscar and Nick's wife Annette's 15-year-old tortoise, 'Morty the Torty'. There is a festive atmosphere when our family gathers; we enjoy preparing food together and laughing, talking and joking and maybe, later in the evening, singing and dancing. The 'Time Warp' from the 'Rocky Horror Picture Show' is an all-time favourite that reminds us we are still young at heart! But beneath the easiness there was a tension as we sought updates on the BOM (Bureau of Meteorology) website and noted the rising wind and rain lashing the windows. Morning revealed a mess of broken tree limbs and torn up shrubs in the large garden and we all pitched in to help tidy up. Not knowing how our house and farm had fared was difficult and we waited several days for the highways from the Atherton Tableland to the coast to be cleared of fallen trees and debris. The first to open was the Kuranda Range road north of Atherton, which added an extra hundred kilometres to our trip home. The further south we drove the more it felt like déjà vu as scenes reminiscent of the aftermath of cyclone Larry revealed themselves—fallen power lines, snapped power poles, houses with roofs torn off and yards and roadsides littered with debris that had once been a something that belonged to someone, thrashed tropical fruit orchards, levelled banana and sugar cane crops and smashed forest. We shared a growing sense of trepidation as we neared our farm and sent a silent thank you to the kind local who had cleared a path through the fallen trees and debris on the road from the highway. We were also thankful for my husband's foresight in taking the chainsaw as he cut a way through the fallen trees blocking our driveway. We drove in, past the house, plastered with shredded-leaf confetti but thankfully intact, and took in the enormity of Yasi's destruction at Quandong Farm.

Yasi was a beast. Our beautiful, natural environment was broken, ripped, torn, shredded, and in the weeks that followed there was a palpable feeling of grieving for nature throughout our community. There was a shared sorrow that we would never again in our lifetime see the local mature phase rainforest as it had been. Many people left. Others dug in and help arrived. Family members lifted our spirits when they came with their swags and supplies and got stuck into the massive clean up alongside us. Thankfully, our decision to remove the greenhouse rain covers meant a lot less damage this time to our hydroponic infrastructure. Resilience was key to recovery. The people of the Cassowary Coast and further afield showed great stoicism and community spirit as they shouldered the load and 'got on with it'. Nature's resilience was inspiring too. Broken and branchless trees soon looked like 'fluffy toothpicks', sprouting new leaves along their trunks. Birds began to reappear, including some species we don't normally see here. Some of us volunteered to chop fruit for cassowary feeding stations, which the Department of Environment set up away from roads and people throughout the region to help sustain the big, flightless birds. These majestic creatures, which grow to two metres in height, have been around for about 30 million years and it is truly a privilege to live among them. Each has a territory and normally roams its patch feeding on fungi and whatever rainforest fruit is in season, and growing the rainforest by spreading the seeds in 'poo fertiliser'.

Eleven years on and the landscape hides its scars well. People have healed too. New homes with up-scaled cyclone ratings have replaced those that needed to be demolished. When our fellow Australians and remarkable native flora and fauna burn in the savagery of catastrophic bushfires in the south and west we feel for them and the locals generally agree: we'd rather a cyclone than a bushfire any day. Or a flood. There have been repeated, overwhelming tragedies over the past few years with mega-floods in the south where the landscape has been deforested. Torrential rain sends water sweeping down rivers and across flood plains and into and over shops and homes with nothing to provide a buffer. The much-reduced rainforest left in the Wet Tropics is thankfully protected by World Heritage listing but astonishingly large swathes of native forest are still being clear-felled throughout Australia. It's common knowledge that such clearing has led to the extinction or endangering of many flora and fauna species in the short time since European occupation of this beautiful land. What can we do? We add our voices to campaigns against greedy, short sighted and senseless clearing of forest that is home and pantry to our native animals, and so important to our planet's wellbeing, and therefore our own species.

The Wet Tropics is our home and we love it here. It gets hot and rains a lot, and mosquitoes can be annoying. When the marine stingers make it unsafe to swim in the warm ocean during the hot summer months, we can always head to refreshing rainforest streams to cool off. We know how to live in this climate. Our houses have insect screens, outdoor decks and wide verandahs, ceiling fans and/or air conditioning. This outdoor living reflects the openness and friendliness that could almost be considered a trait of those who live here. But slowly, slowly the rustic, 'Mission Beach naturally' laidback ambience is evaporating. Climatically unsuitable and oversized houses, many of which are left vacant half the year by owners with a southern orientation, are popping up amid demands for 'progress', with all the busy trappings that will sadly make it just like every other place that has been 'progressed'.

We live in one of the few places on the planet where two World Heritage areas lie side by side. The outstanding natural beauty of Queensland's Wet Tropics and the Great Barrier Reef is just one reason for their inclusion on the heritage list. People come here from all over the world on dream holidays to enjoy and explore these natural wonders in relative safety and comfort. Every year the great tide of grey nomads in their mobile homes washes in when winter begins to bite 'down south' and washes out when our northern spring warms. Up here, there's room to breathe, the flora and fauna are abundant, the beaches are not crowded, and the air and water are clean. It is Sir David Attenborough's favourite place on Earth. Why would I want to live anywhere else?

Magic Carpet Ride

By Sarah Board

I have always been the adventurous type, the possibility of learning more about yourself from the places you go and visit, I'm all about that. As soon as I turned eighteen, I ran, and not to get away from something, but to see what else the world had to offer. Don't get me wrong I love where I grew up, white picket fence, a family who adore me, city life with the hustle and bustle, but I always felt I had things to see, people to meet and places to explore. I'm sure I'm not alone in that.

I had just turned twenty-two and recently returned home from living in London. I had met Alex, someone crazily more unusual and outgoing than me, which is quite rare, trust me. We had only been dating a few short months when Covid-19 took over. We had both lost our jobs, and to my surprise my partner came up with the amazing idea to hire a camper van and travel around Queensland.

To explain, we were both young and we were not all that scared about this sickness that was taking over all the news channels. It was still very early stages, before it had really hit Australia and before any lockdowns. Don't hunt me down.

We travelled from the Gold Coast and had driven all the way to Rockhampton when Alex received a message from one of his mates from university he had lost touch with; he wanted to know if we were coming as far as Cairns and suggested we should catch up.

They invited us to the rural town of Innisfail, which I had never heard of. To be honest, we had the van for another week and I didn't see how we would make it all that way up to Innisfail and drive it all the way back to Brisbane in time. Alex was adamant, and it became a fight. I ended up agreeing. Secretly and silently, I hated that we spent the next two days nonstop driving, when all I wanted was to enjoy the ride and the towns along the way.

When we finally arrived in Innisfail, I was quite surprised at the beauty of the place. It was such a pretty drive and was nothing like what I had pictured in my head. The change in climate, in plants, all in the space of a few hours felt as if we had travelled to a completely different country. Don't get me wrong, the town was dated, a little old fashioned, but it was the countless banana farms, grazing cows and country hillsides that had me hooked.

We were told we had to see Etty Bay. I thought someone was playing a trick on us. We were confused as to how a beach could be two minutes away without seeing any beach in sight for kilometres. Just countless hectares of farmland and hills as far as the eye could see. We travelled up over a hill and once we hit the top, it was a magical moment. The sounds of the sea, the smells of salt and ocean and views of a green, hidden beach paradise all hit at once. Not to mention the cassowaries. I had never seen a cassowary. They are dinosaurs, just look at their huge feet!

We finally met Alex's friend William and his beautiful wife Emily. They were both so warm and welcoming, inviting us into their home. They are the type of people that make you instantly want to thank their parents for raising such beautiful souls. We got talking and I was absolutely shocked to hear how much their house cost them and how cheap the housing was in the area. Locals might not agree but compared to Brisbane pricing it was cheap as chips.

Alex and I looked at each other and it was as though a lightbulb went off at the same time in our heads. That's when our minds took over with the possibility of what a life could look like here. I'm not going to lie; we spent the whole drive back to Brisbane talking about Innisfail. Locals might say I am crazy but it's true. All we could think about was the possibility of owning our own house, years before we thought we would ever be able to. Having some animals and living, not through our phones but through the land. As much as I loved city life, technology is taking over and not for the better. Schools rely on iPad's now to learn instead of using paper and pencils. Kids are growing up playing games on phones and losing their imagination in the process. I am concerned for the next generation.

Alex and I explain Innisfail as being twenty years in the past. It is mostly made up of retired folk, which might explain things a little. For Example, a lot of people still use cash only, schools are as they should be; you learn through pencil and paper and minimal staring at screens. It is a farming town so it's all about getting outside and getting your hands dirty. I was also amazed at the diversity of cultures, which only made me realise how disappointing areas down south were.

Alex and I agreed we both had this pull, an overwhelming feeling that this was where we needed to be. We knew it was a big decision to move and that it wasn't going to be easy, and that we would be making sacrifices to be away from family and friends. It was going to test our relationship, but we felt as a team it was the right choice for us, and we still stand by our decision nearly two years later.

We have both found rewarding jobs. We have saved and bought a house with an amazingly uninterrupted view of the ocean, which I honestly thought only the rich would be able to afford. We have adopted a fur baby and we have been welcomed into the community with open arms. We have been able to achieve more than we ever thought possible at our age, and that's because we took a chance.

I can't say for sure that Innisfail will be our final destination. We are young and love adventure, so we want to travel and explore the world. Our little house on a hill is our paradise and we won't ever want to give up something so special. I can say with one hundred per cent certainty that, no matter where we go, or what countries we visit, we made the best decision to put our roots down here and we will always be back.

Why Should I Stay

By Santina Lizzio

Why should I stay on this land where I dwell?
A gift from my father and his father as well.
As sugar cane farmers they worked this vast land
Cutting the crop, working hand in hand.
Surrounded by mountains, rivers and streams
It's a land of wonder, a land of dreams.

Why should I stay on this land where I dwell?
I'm caught by its beauty, I'm under its spell.
It's engraved on my soul, my heart's in its chains
It nurtures and feeds me, flows deep in my veins.
It's a land of giving and taking as well
I can't help this feeling, want to shout, want to yell.

Why should I stay on this land where I dwell?
It's part of my being, my story to tell.
My ancestors migrated, so long ago
To start a new life, generations to sow.
As the third in that line, I give thanks and I pray
It's my God given gift, so I know I will stay.

Crossroads

By Brenda May

February 1981 – Life at twenty-four

I lay beneath the soft purple cover of my single bed, a small thread of sunlight winked annoyingly as it found its way through a gap in the deep purple curtains. The time showed I still had twenty-seven minutes and ten seconds until a shrill jangle would force me off the bed and into work mode. Afternoon shift, it messed with my body clock and social life. Pfft ... I threw back the covers and jumped out of bed. I had no social life, rather dull, at the age of twenty-four, living in limbo at my parents' house. I pulled my weight with the housework and cooking, paid board, and on day shift, weather permitting, I walked the brisk thirty minutes to work.

Our lives are full of crossroads. A few years earlier, at one of these intersections, I chose a path that led me out of the family nest and into a scenario I felt totally unprepared for. At eighteen and having lived a sheltered life, the party scene hit me hard, I didn't embrace it like I thought I would, and after some disturbing events, I craved the quiet serenity of my parents' house. I returned home after a few months. We won't delve into that pathway, not today. Today we look at how quickly a life can change. How actions and decisions we make shape our future, for better or for worse. See, I knew that first crossroad was a wrong choice from the moment I stepped foot on it, but this morning I had no idea another major crossroad loomed just weeks away.

By rote my eyes flicked to the photo gracing the bedside table. A cloud of emptiness settled over my soul, and I told myself. 'I refuse to look at it today.' Common sense dictated I remove the silent reminder, like an addiction out of control I succumbed to the familiar routine.

I clutched the frame close to my heart, savouring a moment of self-pity before I shrugged it away. Two years later and I knew I needed to move on, but alas, I proved to be a stubborn young lady. My fingers travelled a well-worn path around the deep purple frame, over the protective glass that held a dried red rose framing the rhyme I had written. A simple poem, but the words came from deep within and each time I read them they reinforced my goal never to give my heart to someone again.

He came to me a stranger full of promise and delight.
Patient and loving, he gave new meaning to my life,
He sent me soaring to the sky, I failed to see the danger,
I thought our love was true, he left my life a stranger.

A simple poem, but it looked beautiful with the dried red rose and the neatly handwritten words. He had held out the flower to me on our first date with tender appreciative eyes, and a soft welcoming smile. I think I fell for him at that moment. I was twenty-one and willingly gave my heart into his care. We lasted six months before he left without a word. Inconsolable. To do my poem justice, I bought a calligraphy set and practised for ages before smiling when I finally hit perfection. I put the memory in its place physically and mentally, grabbed my work clothes and headed for the shower.

I felt almost happy with the person who stood before me in the mirror. My body, not skinny, tended to be a little chunky. I struggled with weight gain, but easily lost the excess with a bit of effort. The effort proved to be the hardest part. My best feature curled in all its wildness about my face. Gone were the days of trying to straighten my hair. The early seventies embraced my natural style. With many people paying big money to have the

Afro look, my hair, left to its own devices, did its own thing. Blonde, shoulder length curls, bright blue eyes, a smattering of freckles across my cheeks and a ready smile, made for quite an attractive face.

My stomach rumbled as I strolled into the kitchen. I lifted the lid off the pot bubbling on the stove and took a deep appreciative sniff. The delicious aroma swirled around my nose before fleeing up the exhaust fan. Chicken and veggie stew, my favourite.

"Hey Mum."

"You're up early today."

"Yeah, I woke up before the alarm, but it's ok. Last night shift." I did a little dance around the kitchen, bouncing my hands in the air. "Yay for the weekend. Thank goodness I'm on days for the next two weeks."

"I'll pack up some stew for dinner, and a piece of the caramel slice I made this morning." Mum smiled as I gave her a hug.

I work at General Motors Holden, in the Trim Fab Section sewing the vinyl car seats for the latest Commodore. Mundane factory stuff, but the money is great, and I enjoyed industrial machining. I figured I would stick it out for another few years.

School and I had disagreed with a vengeance. "A pleasant student who tries hard but is easily distracted," my report card repeated itself. On my fifteenth birthday my father said, "if you find a job today you can leave". Which I did. With my school life behind me I thrived in the workforce. Big time manufacturing in Australia created employment opportunities easily obtained. After having five jobs in as many years plus a year at dressmakers' college, I ended up at General Motors Holden (GMH) at the age of twenty-one. Now at twenty-four, with three years in the same job, restlessness started to surface.

I made myself a cup of tea and some toast and joined my father in the lounge where he dozed as the TV buzzed in the background. He looked comfortable with his legs stretched out on a pouffe, eyes closed, and arms clasped across his middle. Dad was a shift worker as well, a Ticketing Officer at TAA, Trans Australian Airlines, and often our paths crossed for this very short time. He wasn't asleep, 'just resting my eyes' he would say, but more than once a light snoring would dictate otherwise.

I munched my toast and sipped my tea watching, but not seeing the program my father had on. An advert for an island paradise flashed on the screen. The Whitsundays, Hayman Island, crystal clear waters and picture-perfect blue sky, people laughing and having a fun time. I sighed, not realising I spoke the words out loud.

"Wonder what it would be like working in a place like that."

"Only one way to find out," my father lifted one eye open.

"As if." I almost snorted into my tea. "Way too far away, a holiday maybe."

I live in suburbia, close to Adelaide, the capital of South Australia. The city life encompassed familiarity. The hustle and bustle of traffic, shops an easy convenience, and being surrounded by constant crowds of people fuelled my security. I got up and kissed my father on the cheek. "Have a good night dad, I better head to work."

I thought nothing more of it as I waited with everyone else for the gates to open and let the flood of workers into the factory. We always stood off to the side while the finishing shift, anxious to leave, had their bags checked. Once done, we could enter.

Having a cheery and sunny disposition, I often found it fun walking through the huge metal sliding doors into the factory with a crowd of co-workers, such a big happy family atmosphere, with smiles and hellos going off left, right and centre.

The worker on the shift before me left my station clean and tidy, but I checked for pranks just to make sure before I sat in my chair. In my section we thrived on playing a trick or two. Things like, removing the needle from the machine so when you started to sew nothing happened. Rigging the chair so it dropped low when you sat, twisting the strong cottons so they broke, and you had to re-thread your machine to start anew. Simple harmless things, like snipping the sewing threads and re-wrapping them around the spindles, it all added to the fun vibe we had going.

Sometimes I would be sent to a different part of the factory. Being a speed demon on the industrial machines, I often ended up where production slowed down, helping get things back on track. Eventually, I became familiar with most of the jobs, and I could be sent anywhere, so I made work friends throughout the factory. I stipulate work friends, as I tended to be a solitary person in my home life. The wild years I'd turned my back on also created a void in friendships, as I broke away from them as well. The two came hand in hand, and as I didn't go out anywhere the opportunity to create new ones never appeared.

The bell sounded to begin work. You did not start before. Start on the bell, finish on the bell. The Worker's Union held strong and enforced their rules. Seven-minute toilet breaks every two hours, even if you didn't need to go. The small ablution facilities would be crowded and filled with cigarette smoke and loud chitter chatter.

I watched the boss walk my way and sure enough today would see me being moved again. Off to the front line where we attached the final pieces on the car seat's vinyl covering, the piping that connected the two halves. It needed a fair amount of concentration, as it must be completely even all the way round. I enjoyed the workstation here, as you weren't surrounded by hundreds of machines. It gave you the feeling of sitting at the front of the class. Sometimes, I had a friend working close to me; we would often pass the busy hours away by writing poetry.

A piece of paper would be handed across the workstation with a single line, sometime later it would be passed back with an added line and so forth. Funny junk for the most of it, but occasionally we would hit a real creative streak. One poem would stick with me for years.

A babe was born
in the early morn,
Tiny fingers slowly unfold
eyes open and behold,
A mother's warmth
A fathers' joy
The lord hath give a baby boy.

Then we did a replacement line.

A mother's warmth
A father's pearl,
The lord hath give a baby girl.

Things like this were fun, but today I worked hard, immersed in my own thoughts as the rise and fall of the constant buzzing of hundreds of machines and a blaring radio filled the factory.

A couple of weekends a month I spent time on my older sister's farm in the country, about an hour from suburbia. She and her husband enjoyed a small lifestyle hobby property, with chooks, a couple of sheep, a few scary goats, a horse and of course a dog and a cat.

The freedom of the drive there felt exhilarating, leaving the city behind, and hitting the wide-open spaces of the Barossa Valley and the rolling hills of grape crops. The first part of the journey consisted of heavy traffic, tooting horns, and traffic lights. Houses, shops, and people going about their daily business crowded the roadsides. Once I passed Elizabeth the main highway became clearer, farmhouses and cropped lands dotted the landscape.

Tomato greenhouses were plentiful, filling the roadside stalls with leftover produce. I pulled into my favourite one to pick up some fresh goodies to take with me.

My car, my pride and joy and trusty companion, happily ate the kilometres to my sister's country home: a beautiful metallic gold, two door Toyota Corolla Coupe and my best friend. I called her Fanny and often voiced my opinions to her as I drove along. She held all my love, sadness, and secrets. February, the weather stayed warm enough for me to wind down my window and let in the country air to refresh my soul.

I loved my weekends in the Barossa Valley. In fact, I enjoyed the wide-open spaces so much that a year previously I took out a loan and bought a block of land at Kapunda. Not far from my sister's farm. Five thousand dollars for an acre. It would take me years to pay it off, but it would be mine. My place to call home.

This time the two days in the country left me restless, pulling an idea constantly invading my head to the foreground, on the drive home I decided to talk to my father about it over dinner tonight.

Mealtimes in our house are always up at the table and a family affair full of laughter and chatter. My younger brother graced us with his presence, which added to the joviality, as we joked and teased each other.

"Hey dad," I said, between a mouthful of crisp roast potatoes and peas. "Remember that ad about Hayman Island? I might apply for a job there, only for six months or so, then work my way back home. What do you think?"

My father put down his knife and fork studying me intently for a few minutes. He rested his hands against his chin as he spoke. "Personally, I think it will be a wonderful experience, but it is up to you to decide what you want to do. It can't hurt to apply and see where it goes."

"That's what I was thinking," I replied. "I mean, I may be unsuccessful."

If anyone understood the restlessness that surrounded me sometimes it would be my father. He, after all, had uprooted his wife and two young daughters and immigrated to Australia from England without a backward glance to the loved ones left at home. I think I may have inherited his spirit of adventure. Except mine was only a tentative two thousand kilometres away, not halfway around the world, with limited funds, no job, and a strange new land awaiting.

Before I could say another word, he continued. "Why stop there, why not do some research and write to all the resorts along the north coast, who knows what will come of it."

My mother glared at him.

Thoughts exploded with excitement. What an interesting concept. "That's a great idea Dad. How many islands are there in the Whitsundays?" Even the name sounded exotic.

"Well, I know of the ones TAA flies to, we can start there. I'll make a call and find out which are suitable to apply for."

"Thanks Dad. I will tackle the application tonight, and hopefully in a few days they will be ready to send."

After dinner I went through my most recent photos. With no time to take another one and wait two weeks for it to be developed, I found the perfect picture. Happy, laughing with a twinkle of fun in my eyes. I wanted to do this right now. I bubbled with excitement. By the end of the evening, I had a vibrant application ready to post. After work tomorrow I would stop at the office shop and get some photocopies done and when the list came together, I would mail them.

The next few weeks dragged by. Two turned into three, then four. I guess my applications ended up in the bin. I was not the sort of person to take off with no security and go apply in the flesh. At least I had tried. I brushed it off, but secretly disappointment took hold. Life continued in the same old pattern. Afternoon shift, day shift, up to the farm. I pushed my attempt to work on a tropical island to the back of my head. Maybe one day, once I had paid off my block of land, I could go for a holiday and investigate what the Whitsundays offered. I set my mind to thinking about my sister's birthday on Sunday.

ell

11th of March 1981 – The crossroad

It was mid-week of my day shift, and my thoughts were on the family get together on Sunday.

"You have a phone call from home. Up in my office."

I jumped out of my skin as the boss spoke. I hadn't seen her approach my workstation. Fear exploded. Dad never rang work. Something must have happened to one of my family. I shook as I followed her up the flight of stairs to her large glass windowed office.

Dad's first words were settling, "don't panic, there is nothing wrong". I sighed with relief. "Can you meet me out the front for lunch. There is something I want to talk to you about."

It proved to be very hard to focus on work as my mind spun into overdrive. What in the heck could he want? What could be so important he couldn't say it to me over the phone or wait until after work? It took forever for the lunch bell to blast through the factory, and for the machines to fall silent.

I headed out to the shady trees on the neatly manicured lawn area in front of the Trim Fab Section. He sat on a bright blue picnic rug spread on the ground with a flask of tea at the ready. I could sense his excitement and he wasted no time filling me in on a phone call he received.

"The Manageress from Dunk Island called and said if you are up there in two days you have a job. It's in the Housemaid Department, cleaning and preparing the rooms for the guests, but it is a good opportunity to spread your adventurous wings. But as always, the decision is yours. No shame if you decide not to do it."

My heart leapt into my mouth, "But I have to hand in two weeks' notice at work ... and which one? And where is Dunk Island? I don't remember sending an application there?" I scratched my head in confusion. Then I remembered a last-minute addition. I almost didn't give it to my dad to post as it was so far away.

"Far North Queensland right up near the base of Cape York, below a town called Cairns." It means you will have to go back to your boss, explain the situation and leave immediately. In two days, you must be up there. That's tomorrow to prepare and Friday you fly." He added, "if you decide to go that is. Take your time." He laughed. "You have till lunch is over."

Oh my Gosh, dare I do it? My mind freaked out. This is huge. Dunk Island, I racked my brain for all I could remember. I came up blank. Could I fit in a library trip to find out more about the place? Time ticked away. I needed to decide.

"Yes." I blurted out. "I'm going to do it." As soon as I said the words, my heart did a flip and excitement exploded throughout my body. Surely if I experienced such joy at making the decision, it was a sign I'd chosen the right crossroad path.

Dad waited so he could drive me home. I didn't have my car as I enjoyed walking to work with the fine weather. Now we were in March, the cold, windy, rainy winter months loomed so I took every opportunity to take my daily walk. I gave him a hug and an excited smile and headed off.

A friend greeted me as I arrived back at the factory. I couldn't contain my excitement and blurted out I intended to leave work immediately and move to a tropical island in Far North Queensland. What an adventure. Her mouth dropped open, and she shook her head in disbelief.

"You're kidding right?"

My eyes confirmed the truth, and I gave her a huge hug. A tropical island with clear sandy beaches, palm trees and water that sparkled in the sunshine - it sounded like paradise.

The boss expressed her sadness but wished me all the best on my new adventure. I paused at the top of the stairs and surveyed my work base for the last three years.

Rows upon rows of industrial machines, people filing back to their workstations now the end of lunch loomed, sitting at their designated places until the bell rang to signify start time. It hit me: I would not be doing this again. No longer would I be stuck behind a machine in a noisy crowded factory.

I walked in a daze back to my station to pick up my personal belongings and said goodbye to as many people as I could. The scene encompassed the surreal, after telling my friend, the news spread like wildfire that I was escaping, moving to a tropical paradise in the north of Australia. As I headed towards the enormous sliding doors the sun streamed through and I felt like I was walking into another life.

As I passed the rows of machines, friends, acquaintances, and some I didn't know stood and clapped and cheered their farewells. Tears trickled down my face and at the entrance I turned to wave goodbye, the work bell rang once more, and I looked up and the boss held her hand up in farewell. Later, when it was released, it would remind me of the closing scene from the movie 'An Officer and a Gentleman', except instead of escaping into the arms of the man I loved, freedom waited as I headed off on a dream adventure of a lifetime.

That afternoon and the next day passed in a whirlwind of preparation and goodbyes. Some friends from work came around that evening and presented me with some travel bags as a goodbye gift. A beautiful suitcase and hand luggage set, I cried anew.

The next day flew by, organising and packing what I thought I would need. Dad had given me a brochure he got from TAA and Dunk Island looked like paradise. For my last night at home we had a family farewell party in the pool room out the back of the house. I danced the night away with my sister between crying on her shoulder. My sister. My best friend, and I would miss her terribly. "It's only for six months," I told her. I intend to work my way back down the coast to home."

Mum and Dad took me to the airport and stayed until my flight boarded. Butterflies performed acrobatics in my stomach. This would be my second time in a plane, the first being a family holiday to England in my early teens. Excitement and trepidation flooded my nerves. For the tenth time I fluffed out my curls and straightened my bright summer dress. I gave my parents the biggest hug, my tears mingling with theirs, and with that I turned my back on my old life and boarded the plane to my new destiny.

ele

Friday the 13th of March – Despair and loneliness

I hated it. I hated everything about the island, and I wanted to go home. Claustrophobic trees and air so thick your lungs needed a ventilator to breathe. It's not that I disliked trees, in fact I loved them, loved everything about the natural world I knew. I guess I preferred the wide-open spaces of the South Australian countryside. My vision was limited because of the forest; it closed around me oppressing my personal space. Everywhere I looked green dominated, every possible shade of green filled my vision, but it didn't make me feel calm like green should. I felt panicked about what the green bushes and trees would hide. The heat overwhelmed me, moist clinging heat that drained my soul.

From the airport, which consisted of a small open gazebo type shed, I was taken to the laundry to meet my boss, get decked out and have a bit of an introduction to my new home. Not so, the boss was way too busy to deal with me, gave me instructions to find the staff quarters and said that the porter would bring my bags when he had finished the guest run.

The staff quarters were well away from the guest accommodation, near the golf course and up a steep hill. There weren't any cars on the island, just work ones, but the narrow road was bitumen and well maintained. It felt a little less claustrophobic as the open golf course enhanced my view, a hot breeze played with my hair, and I realised I could breathe normally again. My nose adjusted quickly to the thick humid air. I started to feel ok, I could do this.

As the staff mess came into view, the living quarters spread out behind it like a sprawling village of connected units. Square white shapes intermingled with the green of the jungle on one side and was more open on the right side to the golf course. Set in neat rows it looked rather appealing as the road travelled straight up the hill through the middle. My block was called the Slink. Room three the Slink. The boss had said it would be the first on the left and the only building below the mess hall, but on the opposite side of the road. What I saw assaulted my eyes.

The ramshackle building I approached was larger than the cosy individual units dotted above the mess. Above the entrance a roughly made sign saying 'Slink,' hung askew and the steady thump of music could be heard within. I shuddered, my heart filling with trepidation. Slightly raised off the ground, the entrance to the wooden building was via four rough steps leading to a large central open area that ran the length of the building. Rooms adorned either side with their numbers above the door frame.

Odds on one side, even the other. A toilet and shower block stood at each end and a large rubbish strewn mess piled in the middle held a mishmash of broken mouldy furniture. The place stank.

I fought back tears; this was not what I envisioned at all. The music stopped and the door to number six opened and a man about my age appeared. He waved hello and called over his shoulder "Welcome to Slink, it's not so bad once you get used to it." My hello in return fell on deaf ears as he sprinted down the stairs and out into the sunshine.

I stood in front of what must be my room. It nestled between numbers one and five but instead of a number it had "THE HOLE" painted in big black letters on the door. Tears threatened to spill down my cheeks. I couldn't handle this, but I had no other choice, the feeling of being so far from home and on my own overwhelmed me. My jaw ached with the tension that had been building since I arrived, and as I went to grab the handle the door swung open, and two ladies came out laughing and joking as they walked.

"Hey." A tall willowy brunette greeted me. "Can't stop or we'll be late for work. Your bed is the one on the end, by the window. Sucks how cramped we are now."

She wasn't wrong. Four messy, unmade single beds squashed side by side, filled the entire room, with barely enough space to squeeze by the bed ends, let alone open the wardrobe doors that graced the wall. My bed, the only one with no sheets or pillow, showed its age by the saggy stained mattress. The thing that grabbed my immediate attention came in the form of a medium sized gaping hole through which I could see into the next room, almost like someone's backside had gone right through it. The occupants must be at work as no sounds could be heard and I certainly didn't want to stick my head through to find out.

Full of despair I sat on the end of my bed and wondered what I had done. What I had gotten myself into. The only window in the room physically touched my bed and trees and thick green scrub filled my vision. Sticky tape, which patched up a small hole in the screen, had started to peel off. I gently pushed it back into place not wanting to make the hole any bigger.

You will not cry. I scolded myself, pushing tears of desolation away. I am not sure how long I sat on the end of my bed. The stuffy heat of the room bought me back to reality. A fan whirled noisily overhead swishing around the stale humid air, making a clicking sound on every rotation. Tick, tick, tick, tick, tick… Once you hear it, it's hard to shut the sound off.

"If you leave the door open when you're in here it will keep your room a lot cooler" The voice made me jump, and I looked up to see my boss standing in the doorway. "Not that there's much breeze today, but it lets the air flow through."

She looked tired; I guess her day had been a busy one.

"Has anyone showed you around?" She asked. "I wanted to bring you up myself, but today has been flat chat."

"It's fine," I lied. "I haven't looked around much, but I will soon."

She shook her dark curly hair. "What in the hell are they doing putting four beds in here? Hang on a tick."

She disappeared and returned moments later. "A couple of the maintenance crew will be along to remove the bed you were sitting on. Sally, who was in the next bed, left this morning, she was meant to bring her sheets down to the laundry." She passed me some fresh sheets and a pillow. "Unless you want that bed, it's a bit worse for wear."

Naturally I chose the better bed.

Two strong men, who I would say were in their twenties hustled into the room making it rather overcrowded. "Sorry about the mix up. So, where do you want this one to go?"

"Leave it in Slink but against the wall near the showers, it will be out of the way there and can be used for sitting on, I suppose."

The men made quick work of removing the bed, and once the three remaining beds were spread apart, it gave the room a little more space.

"Has the porter bought up your bags yet?" He should be here soon. "Let's make up your bed. I'll show you how we do it for the guests so tomorrow you have a good idea before you start."

She was doing all the talking and I was aware I was just giving her the occasional nod or ok. But she was nice and friendly, so it made the situation a little better.

Once the bed was made, she explained there were usually two per room and the waitresses I was now sharing with were moving up to the staff village soon and a new housemaid would move in with me. "Better," she said, "to have people on the same shifts together in the rooms."

We walked a short way up the hill to the building I had seen before, the staff mess. It was large and housed lots of tables and chairs, it was semi open and seemed so much cooler than my room. It had a criss-crossed lattice work door that slid open and closed. A pay phone was by the door we walked in and to the left was a staff kitchen where I could smell the makings of a dinner on the go. The walls were adorned with all sorts of boating and beach paraphernalia. My boss laughed and said "Visiting boaties usually leave behind a piece of wood or shell with the name of their boat on and the boathouse staff bring it up here and hang it. Gives the place great atmosphere don't you reckon?"

She was good at that. Finishing a sentence with a question so I would be obliged to answer. Some tables were also outside under huge trees. A few staff sat around here and there. A couple of the housemaids came in and made themselves a hot drink and said hello.

The boss explained the staffing situation to me. Most newcomers did a couple of months in Slink, sometimes longer, depending on when staff left and rooms in the upper sections became vacant.

"We all go through it. It's noisy and crowded but hang in there. Staff turnover is high, the average person stays one to three months, you will be out of there in no time at all, for some it's only a couple of days." Her accompanying laugh dissipated some of my inner fears and once alone again in my room, I felt slightly more at ease, but I still hated it and wanted to go home.

That first night alone in my room, I felt tired and hungry but couldn't face the thought of going over to the staff mess for dinner.

My inner introvert kicked in big time. I couldn't face using the pay phone to ring home, so I picked up my pen and paper and started to write a letter. The words wouldn't flow, and I didn't want to fill the page with things that would make my parents sad. I found I couldn't lie either; it felt false and wrong.

As I sat on my bed, legs crossed and writing pad in hand, I remembered another time my words felt false, and I was filled with shame. My first year in high school and my English teacher set our weekly homework. We had to write a piece beginning with "Mother packed a picnic tea…" Naturally I left it till the last minute. I couldn't think of a thing to write, in fact I pushed it out of my mind until the morning it was due. I had ten minutes to scribble some lines, so I had something to hand in.

The teacher, I can't even remember her name now, sat perched on her desk, silently reading through the class's homework while we did a writing exercise. When she had finished, she called the class to attention and stated she had one piece she felt compelled to read out. I had my head down, pencil in hand doodling when her words shot through me like shards of ice.

Mother packed a picnic tea, and we set off for no destiny.

Travelling along so fast in our car, we had not gone very far,

when a crash on the roadside we did see, and a man was lying in agony. The moral of this verse is to be very clever, drive a car carefully and live forever.

My hurried scribble poem. I waited for her to laugh and say what a useless jumble of words it was, and obviously written in haste. Instead, she praised it and told me it was a great poem and that I should send it to the Road Safety Council. I remember feeling exposed and fake as she added my name to the end of the poem. I felt twenty-eight pairs of eyes on me boring into my bowed head. I wanted the floor to open and swallow me.

This was the feeling overwhelming me now. If I wrote a happy cheery letter home, it would be as fake as that poem. If I went over to the staff mess for dinner all eyes would be on me, the new person. So, I sat in my room tired and hungry waiting for sleep to consume my fears.

A daily routine over the next two weeks helped me survive. No longer did I wake up and mourn the loss of my love. The framed photo lay in the bottom of my suitcase for a couple of reasons. First, there was nowhere in the room to display personal belongings and two, I didn't want to share it with anyone. The two waitresses I shared with were always still in bed when I got up for work - no way would I expose such a personal side of myself.

Every morning, I would rise at daybreak, a good couple of hours before I had to start work. I would head towards the resort swimming pool and slip silently into the cool waters and do laps. Totally against the resort rules, but I really didn't care, and I formed a silent friendship with the pool cleaner. He would start work just as I finished my laps and give me a shy smile and a wave. I would head back up to Slink for a shower and breakfast before the rest of the staff were awake. Often as I walked over to the mess hall for a solitary breakfast, I could hear alarms going off left, right and centre.

Lunch in the mess with my workmates was enjoyable. A happy group of women who laughed and joked and seemed totally relaxed with life. Many of them were experienced backpackers and world travellers, happy to share their interesting stories. Dinner was served between five and eight, so I chose to head over as early as possible, scoff down a plate of food and head off to a place known as the spit, a long finger of sand down near the jetty where the boats went out to the reef. A good twenty minutes' walk from the staff quarters and at this time of day, it was quiet and peaceful, with the boating activities closed until morning. Every late afternoon I waved at the old boatman who lived in the solitary boathouse dwelling as he sat on his small balcony puffing on his pipe like a seafaring sailor remembering the days gone by.

Shoes in hand, the silky, soft sand, gently caressing and squeezing between my toes, as it moulded to the shape of my feet. Robinson Crusoe-like footprints followed my wake as I walked to the moist sand at the water's edge, letting the slightly lapping waves wash away the day's stress.

The scrubby bushes faded away just past the boathouse, leaving a long stretch of fine sand surrounded on three sides by the ocean. Here you could catch the late afternoon breeze and listen in peace and tranquillity to the sounds of the ebb and flow of the gentle tide.

Why more people didn't come to experience the serenity of the sun sinking over South Mission Beach in the distance was beyond me, but I was glad they chose the comfort of the resort. The sunsets were solitary, spectacular and mine. Vibrant hues of every shade of orange filled the sky. When there were low lying clouds, the colours danced off them turning them into vivid mosaic works of art. The beauty of the moment and my connection with the environment around me bought back a memory of a poem I wrote. My love of the natural world nestled deep in my heart and way back in 1971, I think I knew things weren't going to go too well for Mother Nature. At the age of fourteen I wrote this poem.

Mother Nature
I was once full of beauty,
of flowers, trees, and hills.
But now I 'm slowly dying that greedy man he kills.
He uses my resources, the limit he exceeds,
I can't produce enough to fill his every need.
He clouds my lungs with fumes and smoke
I cannot clear the air.
My rivers once so pure and clean
are now polluted without a care.
Smooth gold and sandy beaches all wrecked with sickly oil,
and deadly things they'll regret taking out my precious soil.
Rockets, cars, planes, and bombs,
you think you're death defying,
But man, you self-destroyer, it's not just me who is dying.
When you've taken all you can, I'll have no more to give.
My pulse will stop its beating,
And man, you'll cease to live.

Proud of my work I posted it to a professional. He condemned it as an immature piece any new writer had to cut their teeth on.

Dejected, I'd put it in my bottom draw and forgotten about it. It was nice to go over it again in my mind.

I took photos of the first of these sunsets to send home. Many times, in the first week I had started letters only to screw them into angry balls filled with negative undertones. Once the photos were developed, I would have a happy, newsy letter for my family to read. I filled a whole photo roll on that first night. Snapping shots of my walk to the beach through the tree laden track to the boathouse. The two-week turnaround from posting my roll of film to be developed, to holding the pictures in my hand, seemed such a long time to wait.

The dirt track leading to the spit and boathouse was wide enough for one island vehicle. No other cars were permitted, except for those involved in guest transportation. On one side of the track the rainforest hug thick and heavy; the other side was lighter with small tempting views of the ocean peeking through at intervals. When the tide was low you could walk the whole way back along the beach to the resort.

By watching the sun sink behind the mainland and the colours fade from the sky, I had to walk back through the dirt track, which was called Sleepy Hollow. Rumour had it that it was haunted, and I was filled with nervous trepidation as I approached it the first night.

"If you are going to come down here for the sunset, you'll need to get yourself a torch." The old boatman swung his weary bones off his patio and accompanied me down the track, shining my way through the trees. "You might step on a snake. There are a few big ones around here, not dangerous though." I appreciated his company and discovered I loved walking at night by torchlight. Sleepy Hollow came alive with shadows and mysteries as he swung the beam about the treetops. It became a nightly ritual with us. I would wave, make my way in solitude to the spit, enjoy the sunset, even though some were way better than others and he would walk me back down the dirt track of Sleepy Hollow. Once I got to know him better, I would often sit for a short while on his little patio before my trek to the end of the spit.

He had some wonderful stories of days gone by and of his time on Dunk, including the island's history. I was fascinated to learn the traditional owners, the Bandjin and Djiru peoples called the island Coonanglebah, meaning, the isle of peace and plenty. I found it romantic and much more appealing than the European connection of being named after George Montague Dunk in 1770 by Lieutenant James Cook. Most intriguing was hearing about Edmond Banfield, a stressed-out journalist given six months to live. He and his wife were the first white settlers on the island in the late eighteen nineties. Together they established a self-sufficient lifestyle and he lived for a further twenty-six years. In the early nineteen hundreds he wrote a book called The Confessions of a Beachcomber, and I put it on my list of things to buy.

A couple of weeks after my arrival, things started to change. I had already decided I must spend the whole six months here before going home. I didn't want to seem like a quitter, but I also couldn't leave earlier and work my way down the coast as planned. It wasn't me, I discovered that about myself, I was not of an adventurous spirit. I arrived back from my trip to the spit, had my shower and prepared for another quiet night in my room when there came a knock at my door. Opening it revealed two of the bar staff who lived in number six. They were a bit shy and flustered when one of them burst out "There is a fancy-dress party in the mess tonight and we wondered if we could borrow some of your clothes. You know, like the dress you wore on the day you arrived." The other guy joined in. "And can you help us get ready?"

I found their enthusiasm contagious and impossible to resist, laughing and joking at their antics. I picked out some clothes and had tremendous fun getting them decked out as ladies of the night. Once they were ready, they laughed and said I should come as their chaperone and get dressed up in some of their clothes. By this time, I was getting a little lonely spending every night in my stuffy room. I had never been brave enough to venture into the mess after dark when it seemed to come alive with music and laughter.

I will be forever grateful to them. I can't remember their names now, they left a few weeks later, but they showed me friendship without conditions, and I am convinced they did it to get me out of my shell and into embracing island life.

_el_

April 1981 – Discovery

From that night onwards my attitude started to change. I still missed my home and family but began to enjoy the Island and its natural beauty. I continued my secret early swims, and my evening journey to enjoy the sunsets and started to discover the island on my days off. A new challenge I set myself on the days I didn't swim incorporated a jog up Mount Kootaloo. Fascinated by the early settlers, I always paused for a moment to pay my respects and read the thought-provoking words on the memorial to Banfield and his wife Bertha, who were buried at the base of the track. I never did make the 271 meters to the top as a jog; it was steep, rocky and way above my fitness level. But walk it, I could. Across the suspension bridge, following the rough, winding root bound track to the top. The spectacular view made the trek well worth the effort. A panorama of the Family Group of Islands nestled in shades of ocean and sky blues, spread out before me. On a clear day the thin line between sky and ocean proved almost impossible to determine.

The island had many beautiful places to visit, and on my days off I would leave in the morning with a packed lunch and be gone all day investigating the wonders. The farm, which produced fresh milk daily; the artists' colony, tucked deep inside the forest housed a potter and a weaver, who built a magnificent dome shaped studio. Their exquisite work was sought after worldwide. Postcard perfect Coconut and Muggy Muggy beaches were beautiful, stunning, and mostly devoid of people. The solitude of these trips appealed to my sense of being. Even sitting on the golf course in the evening produced a spectacular sunset vision.

Most of the things I did on my own, although sometimes I would bump into other staff or guests along the way and a couple of times I managed to secure a vacant spot on a trip out to the reef. I discovered I loved being on the ocean and took to snorkelling like I was born to it, not some city kid too timid to dabble their feet in the sea. The fish and the corals combining to make an amazingly colourful display, stole a piece of my heart and the quiet of the underwater world soothed my senses.

ele

May 1981 – The change

Life was marginally better in Slink after the waitresses moved and a new roommate settled in. Together we made the room more homely. I found a large, discarded picture frame and nailed it over the hole in the wall, it looked silly and out of place, but it did the trick. We found old resort curtains and strung them up over the window. With only two beds we had significantly more room and claimed some of the old furniture that cluttered up the middle of Slink, for bedside tables. But my rose and poem remained in the bottom of my suitcase. As people left, new staff arrived and Slink became overcrowded again. Fortunately, The Hole remained with the two of us. I slowly became sick of the noise and the constant partying all night long in the section outside our room. Being a non-confrontational person, I often lay awake listening to the noise and laughter, wanting to yell out my frustration that I needed my sleep. My room mate could sleep through anything.

After a particularly loud and boisterous night outside my room, I woke up early as usual and prepared for my swim. Outside the door, flaked out bellowing in full snore on a couch lay the main noise maker from last night. To this day I don't know what made me do it, but I grabbed a full jug of ice-cold water from the fridge and slowly tipped it all over his black wavey hair and face. I have never seen anyone move so fast and I reckon his roar of shock woke the rest of the staff. I stood firm and said, "No more partying outside my room." Then horrified at what I had done, I fled from the look of thunder on his face.

That day at work I was in for another shock, The boss called me aside and said a new room had been found for me, if I wanted it. She told me she totally understood if I didn't as it was so far away from the staff quarters and mess hall.

"The boathouse staff have been told to pick a female to live down there." she said, "The place is a mess, and they want someone to help keep it tidy and under control, so it looks better for the guests when they come to use the boats." With a smile she continued. "They have asked for you. The two men will bunk in the same room, and you can have the second bedroom at the back of the house to yourself."

I felt my face split in two with a huge grin and that afternoon I packed my meagre possessions into my suitcase and headed for my new accommodation: The boathouse.

True to their word, the two men had cleaned out the back room. Well, not really cleaned but removed all personal belongings and left me with a double bed, a wardrobe, and a bedside table with a lamp. It felt like The Ritz. Outside the double window less than thirty meters away was the ocean lapping gently against the shore and the cool salty breeze coming through the screens a blessing from the heat.

The old boatman leaned against the doorframe, a gentle smile graced his aged and sea worn face. "It can get stormy at times. The house is old and creaky, but she's a solid old bird. Watch it when it rains, often comes from the nor'-east and can rip through the house all willy-nilly. Shut the louvers and you'll be right."

I drifted off to sleep, the room dark with a twinkling of stars visible through the window. I smelled the freshness of the sea breeze and listened to the rhythmic sounds of the ocean as the flow and ebb of the tide washed and retreated along the shoreline, I felt the happiest I had in a long time. It was relaxing, peaceful and perfect.

My scream as something furry ran across my face bought the men running. The old boatman flicked on the light and with a guilty smile said, "Oh yeah, I forgot to mention we have a bit of a rat problem."

I am pretty sure I swore before he hurriedly continued, "but we wanted you down here. We were told to get a third person in to help clean the place up, and we chose you. You seem to love it down here."

Investigation showed a cute little native rodent hiding under my bed. "Don't kill it." I yelled as he raised a broom. "We need to catch it and put it outside." After much groaning, then laughter and a little screaming from me we managed to get the Fawn-footed Melomys outside. That night I discovered something else about myself. I had a genuine affinity with the native flora and fauna of the island and felt protective of it.

The next day, I exercised my newfound strength and had the carpenters fix up any entry points, particularly the large hole in the shower floor so the house remained rodent free. Within a couple of weeks, the boathouse underwent a transformation. The outside was painted, and repairs were made. Curtains were washed, repaired, and rehung, the kitchen cupboards emptied and scrubbed, my furry little friends evicted, and the open plan two-bedroom house became clean, tidy, and liveable. I took great pleasure sitting in comfortable silence with the old boatman on the small patio overlooking the ocean at the end of the day.

elle

June 1981 – Finding myself

I thrived living at the boathouse, discovering a lot of things about myself with plenty of solitude to soul search. For the first time in my life, I was responsible for my own actions, and it felt good. My letters home took on a happier note as I shared my love of the natural things around me with my family. The sunset photo I took that first night on the spit turned out spectacularly. The mainland of Mission Beach outlined against a plethora of golden orange hues was a joy to behold. I had larger copies made and sent one to my parents and had one framed for the wall at the boathouse.

I enjoyed my job. And found peace in the solitude of cleaning and tidying someone's room for when they returned from a meal or a day out on the reef. I took pleasure in leaving frangipanis or hibiscus flowers in their fruit bowls, the aromas filling their rooms with floral scents.

The staff mess stayed alive with the party atmosphere, but I stopped feeling like I needed to drink to fit in. I would turn up at fancy dress parties as a pregnant teetotaller, or bathroom parties with cream all over my face, curlers in my hair and a nightcap cup of Milo in hand and would see the humorous side of watching other people wipe themselves out.

Young, free, and energetically fit, with dancing blue eyes and wild blonde hair blowing in the wind, I wasn't short of offers to 'hook up,' but I declined. My heart felt mended, but I still had the need to protect it at all costs. I met a man, a tall blonde German with a strong sexy accent. With a shared passion for photography and all things natural we discovered the flora and fauna of the island together.

Our relationship fell into the safe friend category, as he had a girlfriend who was coming out to join him on Dunk at the end of June. He would often walk me back to the boathouse, through Sleepy Hollow in the early evening, our torches searching for any native wildlife to photograph along the way.

I started dabbling in poetry again, simple prose just for myself. On the day he left for a month's holiday to meet up with his long-term girlfriend, I sat on the spit and wept. I hadn't realised how much he meant to me until he was gone. I loved him.

I wrote a simple poem
I cracked an egg on the floor,
it reminded me of my heart by the time he had finished.
I glued it back together again, it lasted for a long
time.
But now I feel it coming apart again,
and this time I think I am out of glue.

July 1981 – The gift and another crossroad

The first week after my German friend left passed in a blur of tears and self-pity before I kicked myself into gear. I had three weeks to pull myself together before he returned with his girlfriend. I would not be a victim. He had never pledged his undying love, the feeling of attraction never surfaced in our long friendly chats. It was purely one sided. We were, after all, friends and I was determined to greet her as a friend as well.

Out of the blue came a gift to lift my broken heart. She was a beautiful blue and white outrigger canoe called Nesmania. She could take two people but handled just as well with a solo occupant. The owner, who I was friends with, always left it tucked up under the boat shed when not in use. He approached me and told me he was leaving Dunk and bequeathed the boat to me on the condition that when I too left the sandy shores, I would pass it onto the next deserving person.

He sat on the beach watching me take it for a test paddle. When I returned from an hour-long excursion out to the neighbouring Purtaboi Island, he smiled. "You'll do," he said, "you're a natural." And with that the Nesmania and I became almost inseparable. Every spare moment I took to the water, sometimes small trips, at others, day long adventures.

One fine glorious morning at the crack of dawn and with two days off, a Canadian friend and I set off to circumnavigate the island. The old boatman nodded and smiled, stowing an emergency pack inside the hull in case we needed it. Other staff were horrified, saying two females would never make it round in a day. We weren't worried, there were plenty of places we could pull into if need be. Paddling with the current, we passed the resort and rounded the point to Muggy Muggy beach. The clear winters day filled us with warmth and the pristine coastline of the island was a joy to behold and refreshed the soul.

We joked and laughed, confessing we were secretly scared our fellow workmates were right and we wouldn't make it and would have to be rescued. We paddled hard and fast and before we knew it, we were three quarters round before we pulled into Coconut beach for a break and some lunch. We made it back in good time before the sun set. The home stretch tested our strength and determination as we paddled hard against the choppy waves and strong current. We could have given up and carried her across the sandy spit, but we were determined to see it through to completion and after we finally rounded the tip of the spit and into smoother waters, I knew I could handle anything life threw in my direction. I felt accomplished and reborn, like I had left all my heartache and worries behind.

Life continued as normal. Work to be done, a boathouse to clean and enjoy and my Nesmania and the ocean as my trusty companions. August loomed closer and with it would come the return of my German friend and his girlfriend. The day before they were due back, my former roommate got the sack. It was a common thing on the island, where the rules were strictly enforced. We called it the three o'clock special. Rule breakers were fired at lunch time and sent off on the next available water taxi to the mainland. Friends and staff would make the trek to the jetty to wave them off and give them the proverbial brown eye as a goodbye.

"Come with me," she encouraged. "We will travel and work the east coast and then I'll show you around my home in New Zealand."

A crossroad again. I felt tempted. We got along incredibly well, and she had way more experience than me in the ways of the world. Life would be drastically different if I walked down that path. And I wouldn't have to deal with the arrival of 'the girlfriend' tomorrow. Somehow, I felt it wasn't my time to leave the island. My six months would be up mid-August, and I had until then to decide what course I wanted my life to take. After a teary farewell, she left for the water taxi. I went back to work in a pensive mood.

She said she was going to hang around Mission Beach for a few days in case I changed my mind and wanted to join her.

Work done for the day, I decided to cook dinner at the boathouse, so I gave the staff mess a miss for the night. I still hadn't fully made up my mind on what I wanted to do. I felt nervous and if I was honest, tomorrow would test the strength of my resolve. Would I be able to cope seeing my German friend with his girl?

I ate my dinner sitting on the sand at the end of the spit, staying long after the stars winked hello in the inky blackness. Deciding to leave my problems for tomorrow I went to bed. Sleep evaded me, thoughts and options ran crazy circles in my head, and I sought refuge in Nesmania and the ocean.

The moon, plump and full hung high overhead, not a cloud in the sky to hide the plethora of vibrant twinkling stars. Moist sand pushed between my toes as I dragged my canoe to meet the glassy stillness of the ocean. The night's embrace felt perfect. A light tease of a breeze kissed my cheek as I pushed off the shore and fluorescent specks of green danced around my paddle as I gently pulled away from land. I rested my oar to drift with the slight current.

A turtle surfaced nearby, her face popping out of the water. Making me jump as she loudly exhaled a puff of air. She drifted with me for a while before she dived below the dark waters. Peace flooded my soul. My heart would survive, and I had an intuitive feeling I wasn't finished with my German friend yet. My decision came as clear as the night sky. I was going to continue down this crossroads path, as far as it would take me. There was still so much to discover on and about the island, let alone the waterfalls, forests, and towns of the mainland.

Maybe for a month or two, or a year, or many, I had no idea. But I realised there was no way I could leave my island when it resonated so deeply with my heart, and the words I had read many times on Banfield's' memorial settled into place.

If a man does not keep pace with his companions, perhaps it is because he hears a different drummer. Let him step to the music which he hears.

As I floated and relaxed close to the shores of Dunk Island, I knew I had found my music.

Licuala Writers' Friendship

By Jean Vallianos

Why did I stay
  So much to say
  You inspired me to write
  To try to get it right.

  Was it your witty jokes
  Or the stories about your folks
  The sad, the joy you had
  The good and the bad.

  I do not like violence
  And prefer silence
  When I do not agree
  With all you tell me.

  Your company is great
  And you tell it straight
  No pussyfooting talk
  I accept it or walk.

  I never have enough time
  But for you I will climb
  That extra mountain peak
  For the truth I seek.

So I will continue to stay
And to God pray
To let you be my guide
And life help me ride.

Stay do not go away
Be with me each day
You inspire me to write
Something happy and bright.

Living my Dream by the Sea

By Penelope Goward

When I was little girl, I lived near a quiet suburban beach in Adelaide. I loved it most in the summer, the clean white sands, and twinkling blues of the water. And best of all in the mornings, when the air was shimmery and salty, before the sea breezes kicked in. I loved the waves splashing to a timeless rhythm, the stillness and peace. Until I came to Mission Beach, I'd almost forgotten how much I loved the seaside. Melbourne can do that.

I moved to Melbourne in my mid-twenties to study and stayed on. Melbourne is an exciting city to live in with lots to offer, and I loved it. I loved the choice of shows and entertainment, music venues, international events, and multicultural events, all the different restaurants, and not to mention the fashion and shopping. I could choose any career I wanted, which I did, several times. I lived in Melbourne for forty years, longer than my time in Adelaide growing up. But as the years went on, and I got older, another side of Melbourne clouded that excitement. The city and suburbs became more congested with people and cars; it took a long time to drive across town, the pollution hovered, and the shows and entertainment became passé. I didn't know my neighbours and I felt the cold. It was cold for nine months of the year, it seemed to me. I'd always said that when you started finding faults in the place you worked, it was time to move on. It also applies to where you live.

My decision to move house with my husband Neil happened quickly at the end of 2017. All our parents had died within a few years of each other, and Neil's daughter decided to move to an exciting post in another country. This meant he and I were no longer the 'sandwich generation'. We could do whatever and live wherever we wanted. I had stopped working full-time and was doing some casual work; I also had several interests and was pursuing them. And Neil, while working full-time, had been planning to move into consulting. He retired when a major organisational restructure was put into place, and he accepted a redundancy package, too good to pass up. I assumed he would put his plans into setting up a consulting business soon after. Neither of us is used to standing still. Change was in the air. He began to reflect past his consulting business plans and started conversations around "what do we 'do' for the rest of our lives?" It seemed that every magazine we read and every conversation we had about stopping work and 'retiring' (whatever that meant), included warnings about the need to have hobbies and interests and corny slogans to pursue your dreams. The superannuation advisers reassured us that it was okay not to work and to enjoy our retirement. But retirement seemed a strange word. What were we retiring from? We were still healthy, with plenty of energy. We just didn't know what we were going to 'do' now that we had all this time and energy for ourselves.

In early 2018 Neil initiated a driving holiday. He saw it as an opportunity to be together to explore and look for a possible new home. This was not good timing for me. I was annoyed at him. Planning a holiday just didn't work for me, and having him around all day in 'my space' made it worse. When I talked to friends and family, they assured me that this was a phase that couples went through, even if you are happy with each other. It's another phase of adjustment to sharing a home-space and being together most of the time.

I realised that I needed to reconsider my ideas. My life was changing. Neil and I talked through my anger at him for suddenly retiring and messing with 'my plans'. Neil was surprised—he had noticed that I had been talking about 'retiring' for quite some time, while he had pictured working for longer. We also talked about our fears for the future. Would we get a debilitating disease? Would one of us get dementia or need aged care? But, during these conversations opportunities and excitement took hold. I also got to see that 'my plans' had been a stopgap to give me activities while Neil was working. I realised that some I could take with me into the future and some I could let go or pursue later. We also agreed that we wanted to live by the sea in a home with sea views, which was a delightful surprise to me. I thought that was only my dream. We considered Melbourne's bay-beaches and seaside beach towns, but they were very expensive, and views of the sea were only across the bay or the sea and perhaps not that interesting. And Melbourne was cold and blustery. The cold is something I prefer to avoid and living indoors during winter was not appealing. We considered other places we had visited in Australia, along the east coast, but again they could be very expensive and were filled with holidaymakers and tourists. Western Australia, around Perth, was also considered. The beaches were clean and sandy with sunset views, but they were too dry and hot during the summers, and very windy. There was only one part of the country we hadn't explored and that was far north Queensland, above the Tropic of Capricorn, where the climate is warm most of the year.

In mid-March we flew into Airlie Beach, to begin our driving trip and see if far north Queensland was a place we could live. The climate contrast was stark. We'd left on a cool morning on the tail end of Melbourne's summer and arrived that afternoon to be greeted by a cloudless blue sky, high humidity, and a temperature of 30 degrees Celsius. The place was lively with tourists dressed in shorts and thongs and wide-brimmed hats, who wandered along the footpaths and peered in shops as they clutched melting ice creams. Bars and restaurants blared their jazz and pop music. Stylish, modern apartments, pressed against the hill, with outlooks across the sea, loomed overhead. You'd never know that Cyclone Debbie had ripped through the heart of this place the year before. We did all the touristy things like snorkelling, exploring local islands and eating fresh seafood. The town people were friendly, and it had a seaside atmosphere, but it was not our scene. Too busy with people and too touristy. We were happy to drive on.

When we first drove into Townsville we were struck by the enormous hill near its centre. It looked dry, dusty, and empty. What we knew about it was from brochures, family, and friends. Over the next few days, we explored the middle of the town on foot and visited colourful street art and historical buildings, had sunset walks along the beach esplanade and ate at local cafes. We took the ferry to Magnetic Island and thought about buying a house there too. We liked Townsville and the island, but we left unsure if it was for us. We'd lived in a large city and suburbs and wondered whether this would be more of the same. So we drove further north about three hours, to a coastal series of villages called Mission Beach, half way to Cairns.

I'd only heard of this town through an acquaintance who had a friend who worked there as the local physiotherapist. He visited once and loved it. He was most surprised when I told him we were visiting, as most people in Melbourne had never heard of the place. My husband had visited Mission Beach on a holiday with his daughter two years before, and was entranced by its untouched beaches, rainforests, quiet community, and beachside houses. He noted that the population was around 3000. Nice and small. We stayed in what is known as 'north Mission' or the main town in a beachside Queenslander up on stilts, in walking distance to cafes, restaurants, and shops. There was a long white beach nearby, dotted with coconut palms and patterns in the sand made by tiny crabs. And views of Dunk and Purtaboi islands, and Bedarra Island in the distance. Our walks were tranquil and even the rain was warm. It rained a lot as it was the monsoon season. I'd never experienced such a deluge. Like water pouring from the sky, pressing down on leaves, drumming on roofs, leaving puddles and pools everywhere. The rain hissed and steamed on roadways, and it was hot and muggy. The air-conditioner in our Queenslander got a work-out.

To amuse ourselves because of the rain and to satisfy our curiosity, we arranged for a local real estate agent to show us some properties. Steve, from one of the real estate offices, was pleased for the company, and as he drove around, he delighted us with stories about the history, local personalities, and his own life in the area. He had been previously married to local artist, Helen Wiltshire, who had died too young and how he had lived with her and their three children on Bedarra Island. The area has attracted artists of all kinds and had been like this for over a century. For example, the famous John Busst who in the early twentieth century considered himself an artist but is more well known for his work as a conservationist. He led a successful campaign in the late 1960s to protect the Great Barrier Reef from mining and exploitation and worked towards preserving the tropical rainforests from development. Other notable artists, such as: the Cohen sisters, Noel Wood, Deanna Conti, Jenn Payne, and Bruce Arthur who set up an artist's colony and gallery on Dunk Island, which was later managed by the artist Susie Kirk after his death.

Steve showed us houses that ranged from run-down, precisely designed, old and new, and well within our budget. None was facing the sea and only some were near the beach. We were curious—what would an expensive house cost and look like in this area? He rummaged through his offerings. His face lit up, a gleam in his eye. "I have a couple of places in mind", he said. One house was on the beach and called a 'pole house', because it was built around wooden poles that looked like they could prop up telephone lines. It was dark timber and seemed higgledy-piggledy, on three levels and rooms scattered throughout the house with joining corridors. The next house he showed us was painted white and nestled amongst tropical vegetation, with steps to the beach, and a new deep-blue-tiled swimming pool. Sea breezes stirred the air. It was a beach house, with open windows and shutters, all facing the sea, and views of the islands. We were instantly in love with what we called 'The White House' and were seduced by the fantasy of living there.

Steve was delighted for us but explained it might be outside our budget, given the prices of the other houses we had looked at. It was. Later that day, we looked at our finances and knew we could afford it with a little bit of manoeuvring and rang our bank manager in Melbourne. But it was the Easter holidays, the banks were closed, and the owners were away on holidays too, so the completion and signing of the 'offer' couldn't be done. The paperwork was one step from the final signing and contract to buy. We were very disappointed. We would have to wait until after the Easter holidays. We were returning to Melbourne in a few days, quite possibly it would take even longer, because negotiations would have to be done through email, the real estate agent, and postal services.

Our accommodation was booked and paid for in Palm Cove, several hours drive further north. Reluctantly, we left Mission Beach leaving our White House behind. As we drove, with only the road and scenery for company, we talked about our love of The White House, but nagging doubts crept in. What if there was another cyclone? Would we be safe? What about insurance? What about living so close to the beach? Are the council rates higher? What had we fallen in love with? Was it more of a beach-house rather than a house to live in? It didn't seem to have much storage. Would everyone going to the beach look in? We were beginning to see beyond the whiteness.

The weather was sunny and warm in Palm Cove on the first day. We sat on our balcony sipping cold beers, our conversation returned to the White House and our doubts, and that there was one house we hadn't visited in Mission Beach. It was a house that was on the bottom of a list we'd put together weeks before that perhaps we might look at while we were in the area. Could we be bothered driving back to Mission Beach from Palm Cove? And later that day, when we looked at the house on 'Google Maps' or 'Street View', it looked like a steep walk from the garage to the house. My immediate thought was of carrying shopping bags up that hill, no thanks. Then the rain returned, and we couldn't go out exploring

Palm Cove, so we decided, for something to do, we would drive back to Mission Beach and see this house.

The next day was Easter Sunday, everything except cafes and restaurants were closed, and the chances of a real estate agent picking up the phone that day were slim. I rang anyway. A woman's voice answered, warm and friendly. She explained that it was no trouble to show us the house, even during a holiday weekend. She couldn't have shown us earlier because she had been away. We made an appointment for the following afternoon.

The next morning the sun was shining. We drove nearly three hours to get there from Palm Cove. We laughed at ourselves and our impulsiveness. What were we thinking? Our image of ourselves was of middle-class, educated, stable Melburnians. What were we doing considering moving to this part of the country? We had no answers, and did it really matter, we said to each other. Our only concern was whether we could find a house and preferably by the sea. Did it exist? I thought of my peaceful beach as a child. Was I ever going to capture those moments again?

We met Lynn, the real estate agent, at the front entrance to the house. It was another 'pole house' on two levels, built twenty years ago by the current owners. Immediately my shopping bag fears were 'put to rest'. The property had two road entrances, and the garage was next to the house on the top road entrance. She showed us a sparkling swimming pool, landscaped with rocks and garden furniture. Lynn laid out the site plans on the outdoor table. We looked at each other with puzzled looks. "Oh no!" I thought, she's trying to tell us that this is the best part of the house. We walked down into the steep garden, which was full of luscious green, yellow, and red tropical shrubs and tall palms. Even though the garden had been landscaped lovingly, I still wondered why she wanted to show us the plans and garden first? Neil kept quietly nudging me with puzzled looks too. We didn't see this as a good sign of what was to come. At last, we came back to the front door. Large, and made of solid timber and an old-fashioned keyhole, like a door on one of those old wooden ships. Lynn opened the door.

When we stepped into the house we gasped. The view across the sea to the islands was vast: every shade of blue, soaring birds, waving palms and white sands—all from an expansive and airy verandah. The house itself was a family home, modern and comfortable, with lots of different timbers. Sailing ships and sailing artefacts decorated the walls. There were three bedrooms, enough for guests to stay in and one to take over as a study of sorts. It had large entertainment spaces and two wide verandahs, on two levels, with 270-degree views across the Coral Sea and the valley beyond the Hull River and the little village of Carmoo, and an outside patio covered in purple and pink bougainvillea. My fears of being blown away in a cyclone were diminished too when I saw the built-in bunker and learnt that the house had survived two high-category cyclones. We were dazed. An enormous view and a short walk to a white-sanded beach, all within our budget. The 'White House' faded away. This wasn't a beach house but a home. We signed on the spot! It was the end of March, and we moved to Mission Beach on Boxing Day, at the end of the year. But much happened in between.

The fullest year of my life was in 2018. In project management language, we were on the 'critical path'—there was no time to spare.

We returned to Melbourne determined to sell our home. Our 'to do' list was extensive: we had to engage a real estate agent to sell our home, declutter and repair aspects of it ready for sale, store most of our furniture, and find a suitable removalist. In the end, we sold quickly because of where we lived and the current economic climate. But it was the decluttering process that took most of the time. We had lived in it as a family home for over fifteen years. The amount of 'stuff' we had collected from travels, family members' gifts, sentimental keepsakes, and personal hoarding was astonishing. It took three months to go through everything, give it away, pass things on to family, and throw out what we could see was junk or rubbish. Little did we know we would continue this process several times when we arrived in Mission Beach—because the lifestyle is simpler, and the climate and houses are different.

Plus, Neil and I were teaching English in China for a month over July, and we had to prepare our educational program for that. Lastly, we had to finalise our planned three-month tour to Spain, Portugal, and Morocco in early September. We worried that we had taken on too much. We had. However, thanks to friends in Melbourne, it was made possible.

We arrived in Mission Beach after having driven from Melbourne over eight days. Family begged us to stay for Christmas celebrations, but we really wanted to settle into our new home in South Mission Beach.

On arrival at our home, once again, we were entranced by the view and felt appreciative of how lucky we were to find the house of our dreams in the tropics, by the beach, with a swimming pool. The house came with furniture, including beds and mattresses, so we could start living here immediately. We thought in a few days our personal belongings would arrive, but that was not to be. It was also the wet season, so the wind howled, and it poured with rain. We had never experienced horizontal rain. Fortunately, there were no cyclones forecast although there were threats off the coast. We wouldn't have known what to do anyway. And, except for our closest neighbours we knew no one. We set about exploring the local area and what it had to offer. There were a few restaurants and cafes, a chemist shop, minimal medical services, a large supermarket, some art galleries, and a local pool. We wanted a quiet neighbourhood away from the noise and bustle of the city too. Our closest neighbour was 100 metres away, and Cairns was a two-hour drive. For us, this was paradise.

The honeymoon was quickly over. The first few months were challenging as we adapted to the hot and humid weather. We discovered that there was only one air conditioner in the house, working fans but they were old and caused rust spray-marks around the walls, and only a few insect screens on windows and doors. The previous owners were well adapted to the heat and insects, but we were not. To our dismay our furniture and belongings had not arrived from Melbourne. We discovered that the removalist was probably not honest. Our belongings did arrive eventually over several months, trickling instalments on different removalist trucks. We heard other stories of shonky removalists, stories of others who had paid thousands of dollars to have their furniture and personal belongings sent here, only to discover that some had not arrived or were broken. We reckoned we were lucky that our stuff had arrived at all. Then, living in the house, we began to see some shortcomings. It certainly was a strong house, but it needed maintenance—in the tropics maintenance is every few years not fifteen or twenty years. It was also dark inside, the interior design was dated, and there was little or no storage. The internet was also not working despite frustratingly long phone calls to the telecommunications company, wasting their and our time. We needed to find another way, which we did, quite by accident. We discovered that another company had a telecommunications tower on the nearby hill, what insiders call: 'in line of sight'. We now have the fastest internet in town. But I was depressed. What had we done? Left our family and friends, the comforts of living in Melbourne and the known. To this! I soon recovered as I became involved in local activities and community groups, thrust upon us in a way, because of a surprising global event.

To our surprise and dismay, one year after moving to Mission Beach a worldwide pandemic struck: COVID-19. We were extremely lucky to be here as it turned out. We experienced little or no lockdowns, our closest neighbour was 100 metres away, we had the beach to walk on and meet and chat to people, lots of fresh sea air, and socialising was mostly outdoors. Mission Beach is also classed as a remote community, and it was only at the very end of the two-year federal and state health restrictions that we had to wear face masks inside when we shopped at the supermarket or chemist. We knew no one with COVID-19 except some friends and family in Melbourne and Sydney. We were a community that was relatively untouched by restrictions or COVID-19. If we had stayed in Melbourne, we would have had to endure nearly two years of restrictions and would have been confined to our house. Quite a contrast. However, the pandemic did stop us from travelling overseas but we could travel around the state of Queensland. We visited outback Queensland and Cape York. Something we had dreamed of doing but it was brought forward and made a reality during this time. We were very lucky to be able to travel and visit interesting places. If we had been in the state of Victoria, it would not have been allowed or possible. Three years later, we are only planning to travel overseas now that vaccinations are available for the majority. The pandemic also meant we could renovate our home, which we did.

The pandemic closed us off from most of Australia and because there was no international travel it meant we had some 'spare change'. We decided that our home needed to be updated and we commenced renovating the parts of the house that bothered us the most. The house is on two levels including two wide verandahs or decks on both levels that make the house look rounded and extend the house on the east side towards the sea. Some people referred to it as the 'flying-saucer' house. The kitchen, entertainment area, two bedrooms with a main bathroom and an ensuite bathroom for one of the bedrooms and an outside pool are on the upper level. The lower level is joined by stairs and has a bedroom, a sitting room or lounge, a bathroom, and an extensive verandah. We decided to start with one of the upstairs bedrooms that had an ensuite bathroom to make it into a dedicated guest room. We realised that having the downstairs bedroom as a guest room wouldn't work. We imagined it could be difficult for guests to lug suitcases, and elderly family and friends to walk up and down the stairs. We decided to relocate the master bedroom suite downstairs instead. That way we would be using the whole house. So, our renovations began. Over time it became clear that once you start renovating it's hard to stop, and fortunately for us we had the money. The house, over a three-year period, was completely transformed from dark to light and reworked, and all the maintenance and restoration issues that needed repairing or replacing were done. Exhausting but satisfying work. The house was transformed from an ordinary pole house to a house with character and all the latest mod cons. The house with a 'million-dollar view' became a 'million-dollar house'.

So why have we stayed? It is only now when we look back, that we realised it was a brave move and how big that move was. We went through the list: we were newly retired (whatever that meant) from working full-time, we had moved interstate from a city lifestyle in Melbourne to thousands of kilometres away to a rural and coastal lifestyle, from a cool dry climate to a hot moist climate, and from a house in the suburbs to a beach-house on the coast. Besides, we knew no one when we came here, and we didn't know what Mission Beach could offer or what went on. Very brave indeed!

I remember when I changed my driver licence from the state of Victoria to Queensland, something one is required by law to do within three months of arrival. I saw in an instant that I could no longer identify with being a 'Melbourne-ite' or a Victorian. There was a new address and even the colour of the licence changed from green to goldy-yellow. I was shocked. I hadn't realised the impact of this small act. I was no longer a 'Mexican' because we had lived south of the border, but now a 'banana bender'. I felt depressed for weeks. My identity had been challenged. I needed time and space to think about who I was again.

In those first few months while we settled in and waited for our personal possessions to arrive, we sold or gave away some of the furniture in the house and bought new furniture we liked. It turned out to be a great way of meeting the local people and we formed an instant friendship with one couple who lived nearby. But there was a standout experience. It was an extremely hot morning as perspiration trickled down our faces and necks. He came from Cairns with his pet parrot to purchase a corner unit to display memorabilia about his mother. He talked non-stop about her photos and personal items, and how much he missed her. All the while the parrot played. The parrot was bright green with a sharp red beak, bright eyes, with a very knowing air. It was quite used to being the centre of attention and loved it. The bird sat on this dear man's shoulder and nibbled his ear, walked up and down, danced, and jiggled, licked the perspiration, and happily called out loudly with gurgles and trills, whistles, and squawks. The parrot was mesmerising. We couldn't keep our eyes off it, and we tried desperately to listen to this man recounting his memories of his mother. It was hard not to laugh at the bird and insult this grieving man. After about an hour or so of talking, he gave the bird some water, picked up his corner unit and put it in his trailer, and headed to the beach to collect white, chalky, cuttlefish bones for the parrot. We laughed heartily when he left, not at the man, but at the bizarre situation—something we had never experienced before.

Neil and I jokingly describe Mission Beach as an 'un-gated retirement village'. It seems to attract the retired, who are looking for a beach holiday residence that is friendly, quiet, and a warm place to live. But it also has lots of families who live here because of work, the primary school and location by the sea. Mission Beach is divided into five villages, all sharing the postcode '4852': Bingil Bay, Mission Beach, Wongaling Beach, South Mission Beach and Carmoo. It has many accommodation places, no fast-food chains, one large supermarket, several cafes and restaurants, one physiotherapy clinic, one chemist, and a half-hour drive to the closest hospital. Sadly, the local doctor departed to join a larger practice in a nearby town, which means that residents need to drive at least half an hour to two hours (Cairns) for a medical service. We also must drive everywhere, as there is no local bus service. We began to realise that this was not going to be our 'forever home'. As we age, with no family support, and the two-hour drive to Cairns, we would have to leave our little patch of paradise and live back in a town with more medical and support services. Probably in Cairns, in a manageable apartment. But, who knows, this may alter in the next few years as Mission Beach changes and more facilities become available.

Mission Beach community is welcoming, most people are from all parts of Australia and some from New Zealand. Some are from families in the surrounding country towns, sugar cane farms and banana farms who own beach houses in the area. We have discovered many other Melburnians living here, and even from my home city Adelaide, including a friend who I went to school with briefly and discovered our mothers used to work together, and a woman who trained as a midwife in Melbourne at the same hospital as myself, both well over forty years ago. We also discovered that Mission Beach for retirees can provide a full life. I can't say the same for young people, unless you've gone to school here and know friends that way. For us there are community events to be involved in like market days and social occasions. We joined a social group that eat out at the local restaurants which is fun to participate in, and from there we discovered people who live near us who enjoy meeting up at the beach for a picnic and a social chat. Neil was invited to go fishing with male friends out to the islands and the Great Barrier Reef. I suffer from terrible travel sickness, including sea sickness. I won't tell you about the disgusting stories of my unfortunate experiences. He brought back fish we had never heard of or seen before. Mission Beach Community Arts Centre turned out to be more than a gallery, and I participated in art workshops and got to know people that way. Neil became the president of Mission Arts, as it is commonly called, and found many like-minded people there too. I joined two book clubs where we discuss books and socialise—I sometimes wonder if the socialising isn't more important. I discovered a writer's group in the region that has a long history of local writers and publishers and found many likeminded people who share the pleasure of reading extensively and writing. I joined the local Mission Beach historical society, where I contribute as part of the committee, and I helped set up the administration structure. I also have had the privilege of interviewing a few local artists in the area, so their stories could be told and recorded, and not lost. But it was when I joined the aqua aerobics group at the local pool and a yoga group that my friendships expanded and deepened. I discovered more neighbourhood friends and my coffee mornings after the sessions expanded to lunches, dinners, and social events. For two people who knew no one and had little or no expectations of the place, in a short time we were busy with community responsibilities and social activities. Never a dull moment!

Living in paradise means family and friends visit from the colder parts of Australia mostly during our winter. They see it as a holiday. I see it as work. Lots of preparation and then cleaning up afterwards, plus feeding and entertaining them while they are here. Not many people like the heat and humidity, which is six months of the year, and prefer to visit in the winter, for them it's like summer. For us, because we have acclimatised, winter is cold when it goes down to 18 degrees Celsius overnight and 23 or 24 degrees Celsius during the day for about two or three months of the year. We had many families and friends to visit in our first year, during the winter, before the pandemic, and only a few since. In the beginning I was excited to show them our house and garden, the villages of Mission Beach, cassowaries, and tourist spots. But since then, we've visited many of the places they want to visit, and often several times with previous guests or just on our own out of curiosity. We also have our routines, friends, community responsibilities and things to do, and so they do not always understand that these need to be put aside when they visit. We encourage them to bring their own car or hire a car so they can explore on their own. But at times we feel like a hotel, providing a bed and meals. We've had a few wonderful guests, who stay only a few days, have ideas of what they want to see and discuss their ideas with us before they come, help around the home, contribute to meals, enjoy our company and leave a gift. But, as the saying goes: "Guests are like fish, they go off after a few days!" I agree.

We look back, as we enter our fourth year, after three years of settling in and making new friends, house renovations plus the maintenance, all during a pandemic, and we have realised that the changes have gradually had a cost. We are mostly tired of moving around our house as each section was refurbished, and all the builders and contractors walking in and out as they worked. We are glad to see it all come to an end. There's still a bit to be done, but nothing major. Fortunately, Neil enjoys repairing and building projects around the house, so they will keep him busy and fulfilled.

We are also tired from the effort of moving interstate, meeting new people, adjusting to the climate, and learning about the local area. We sometimes reflect upon a fantasy we had about living in Spain. What we now know is that would have been an even greater effort, with the change of culture, language and housing to name a few, and the pandemic would have stopped us from returning to Australia for years, which perhaps could have taken its toll in lots of subtle ways. A recent trip to Melbourne for a family wedding in the early part of winter confirmed that we had made the right move. It was cold, overcast, congested with traffic, and polluted. Great city to experience and visit, but no longer to live in. Moving from Melbourne to Mission Beach was the best.

I'll keep exercising at the pool with friends and contributing to the Mission Beach community and we'll do some more renovations around the outside of the house. We'll plan holidays to visit family and friends and for sure they will visit in return. We have our dreams to tour around Australia on driving holidays and travel abroad. And we have come to accept that we won't be able to live here for ever, but for now Mission Beach offers a lifestyle for us, the 'healthy retired', that is social and active in a warm climate. And I can live out my dream by the sea all year round.

Relief

By Jacque Duffy

Green blue hue
   droplets bounce
   with relief in view
   umbrellas announce
   a wet overdue
   the heat to trounce.

Seven Reasons Why

By Jeannette Smith

I bought my house in Mission Beach in November 2017. Widowed, in my sixties and with no family closer than 2000 km away I was—and still am often asked—why Mission Beach?

There is always a moment of silence following this question—how much do I share, will you think I am crazy if I tell you exactly how I ended up here. If I consider the question to be merely polite, I often respond with 'my husband and I always intended to settle in this area' and go on to say how happy I am to be here. Sometimes, however, that is not enough. The person asking the question has displayed a genuine interest; it is not just idle curiosity. Even then, I stop to think. So, no—It is so much easier to tell you why I stayed. With a little help from the Blog I use to keep in touch with my sons, let me start on the most obvious reason.

I stayed because I love the beauty of Mission Beach

I stayed because of the environment, the climate, the consistent temperature range. I stayed because of the deep blue colours of the reef on a sun filled day; I stayed to watch the sun rising over the islands and to watch it create an amazing pallet of colour in the sky setting at day's end. I stayed because I could see the stars and planets from my deck at night. I stayed and listened to the water hit the shore as the tide came in. I stand with doors wide open, letting the wild storm winds whip my hair. I stayed because I felt the rainforest embrace me.

'Pre Dawn Over the Barrier Reef'

The sun hasn't risen yet, but I am already absorbed by the sights and sounds about me as the sky lightens. The door to my verandah is open, and so are the wooden window shutters. The air is refreshingly crisp and cool. According to my infra-red clock it is 75 degrees F. Every time the power goes out, the readout reverts from Celsius to Fahrenheit. Above the noise of the active birds, I can hear the raucous laughter of a kookaburra. I love living here! As I have been writing, a large black cloud has drifted in over Dunk Island. That will add depth and contrast to the sky when the sun emerges.

I have always been aware of, and grateful for, the struggles of the environmental groups who fight desperately to protect this region from aggressive, inappropriate development. If it wasn't for their insight and courage in the face of extreme antagonism, much of this natural beauty would have already disappeared.

'Partly Cloudy, High Chance of Showers'

I am feeling a weather bond with those in cooler climates this morning. Weatherzone forecasts a day of showers and some cooler temperatures. As I write, it is 24.5 degrees C.

The term 'showers' has to be taken in local context. The showers were heavy enough to wake me in the early hours of this morning, but I do concede it wasn't a continuous downpour. More of a stop-start affair. The verandah boards are wet, so there has been a strong 'breeze' behind it. At a guess I would estimate only half the annual rainfall expected at Wamboin [a semi-rural area in NSW, just outside the ACT border], for example, fell.

The local birdlife (and in this group I am including my neighbour's three red hens) appears to be loving current conditions. The little yellow sunbirds are quite chatty in fact. I don't believe in caging birds and the exuberance displayed by these tiny creatures reinforces my view. They come and go as they please, treating the verandah as their own space. They have so far constructed three nests in my garden. The one hanging from the grevillea outside my office window is a motley looking affair. It swings precariously in high winds, so perhaps that is why adult sunbirds are hyperactive. They bring much joy to my mornings when I sit outside at the table, eating my breakfast, writing or reading. I can't see the curlew family from this angle. More than likely they are standing statue still at the edge of the garden path, balancing on their long spindly legs. If someone were to walk along there, these creatures would emerge serenely and glide unhurriedly to another section of the yard where the plants provide both camouflage and shelter.

'About Our Rainfall'

This just came in from the Mission Beach Community Association newsletter, which keeps the locals updated on things happening within the village. "First day of 300 mm rainfall for 29 years. 20 May 2020: 302 mm recorded in BOM gauge at Bingil Bay (privately monitored). The last time we had 300 mm plus in a day was February 1991: two days: 435 mm and 306 mm. Time before was in January 1981 in the biggest rainfall month for us on record since 1926. "Year to date we were 800 mm behind our average year's rain at the end of April. We are catching up but still well below normal Wet Season. Ken Gray" No wonder I needed to empty excess water from the swimming pool many more times on Wednesday than any other day since I moved here.

The Wet Tropics and surrounding areas - the Reef and the Tablelands - are impressively beautiful. I am a photographer and my eyes register the details. The colours are extraordinary, the tonal variations, the textures, the contrasts all appeal to me and I never take them for granted. They appear new and fresh to me every day. I wanted to share this with the boys. Now I want to share it with you.

'The Road Less Travelled'

The weather has been superb, so like everyone else in the area, I have been out and about enjoying life to the max. Several times recently I have needed to travel to Innisfail and have taken the long way there and back. It adds significantly to my travel time and mileage when I detour, but as I pass through some of the most magnificent scenery in Australia, I don't consider that time wasted. I rarely take my camera with me, so I have missed out on some stunning photo ops. However, you don't necessarily want to be taking that gear with you to appointments in town.

As the beautiful sunny days seem to shorten, and the longer, grey days of the Wet Season come upon us, the possibility of cyclones occurring seems to be on everyone's mind: particularly concerning to those people who live down south rather than up here. For people in the Wet Tropics they are simply a fact of tropical life. Newer residents like myself probably look to the skies more often than the old timers. Trudy Tschui once told me the time to take earnest action was when those who had lived here all their lives began to move the outdoor furniture from the verandah. Good advice!

'Hey Rain'

Yesterday, as the rain continued to fall, and I was getting soaked emptying excess water from the swimming pool, I found myself singing this old ballad from 1999: Hey Rain. It was actually written back in the 1940's, but the version you probably recall is the one that was always playing on "Australia All Over" on the ABC. It is the one about all that rain falling on your hands and face. It is a song about the wettest place in the Southern Hemisphere and mentions a number of places within a 50km radius of Mission Beach. Who would have thought then that I would ever be living it?

In the first twelve months after moving to Mission Beach, I made five road trips to the ACT and Gold Coast to finalise matters relating to three Estates I was administering as Executor. While down there I was touched by everyone's concern for my welfare:

it's so wet up there, there's so many cyclones, it's so isolated, it's so hot, it's so humid, there's so many insects, it's so far away. You're on your own. You're so far from your children and grandchildren. And so it went on. Thankfully crocodiles didn't get a mention.

What I realised a long, long time ago was that you can focus so much on negative aspects of where you happen to be living, the truly amazing things about that place could be missed. When I first left Sydney - Manly/Seaforth - to live and work in western NSW, there were times I missed my family, friends and lifestyle so much that a huge wave of homesickness would sweep over me and I would drive myself to what was then a demarcation speed sign on the edge of town. I would sit and look at the direction signs, trying desperately to stop myself from continuing down the track. The Eagles 'Hotel California' had just been released and the last verse in particular resonated with me. The verse about checking out but never leaving: that was exactly how I felt.

It may simply be that I am much older now, but that country town was not quite as friendly or welcoming as Mission Beach has been to me. But I did come to love it and, dare I say it, it loved me: eventually! I flattened all my North Shore vowels and joined every organisation I could. I was second lead in the local amateur drama society; I taught Sunday school; I was a member of the Art Society; I studied accountancy at the local TAFE; had fun at work. I was the local racing photographer. The more I got to know the people, the more I got to know the environment (our office was responsible for 43% of the State's health care at the time) and discovered for myself what an amazing place it really was. However, my future was never there, and I eventually moved on to other equally interesting places.

As I said before, it is nice to know my southern friends are concerned for my safety here, but I wish they wouldn't worry quite so much—given the places and experiences I have survived in the past. Fortunately, the Wet Tropics haven't had to face the terror associated with bushfires. During the Canberra Fires that happened 20 years ago, I was a communications volunteer in the Regional Disaster Centre of the NSW Rural Fire Service, and like many who worked around the clock for so many weeks during that emergency, I later experienced Post Traumatic Stress Disorder. It caught most of us unawares: we knew we had been working in the eye of a crisis, but it wasn't until sometime later, when Coroner Ron McCleod was releasing his findings, that some symptoms which had begun to manifest themselves, could be linked to the event. I am fortunate because mine have faded over time, although helicopters flying overhead can still cause my nose to think it can detect thick smoke. One part of my brain knows it's not there. Another part still reacts. Several of the men I worked with during this crisis actually succumbed to heart attacks within 12 months of the fires. Given my responsibility at that time, I got off lightly.

I experienced small cyclones (Category1 and Category 2 levels—where windspeed reaches around 83 knots) while living in Darwin, and two severe, destructive tornados around the Bungendore NSW escarpment, but they never triggered the emotion within me that fire can. Several years ago there was a small fire along the Tully Road. As soon as I had smelt the smoke, I had my evacuation plan activated—including having a woollen blanket folded at my front door. Neighbours assured me I was in no danger and today I no longer worry.

No-one knows how they will react in an actual emergency. There must be people here in Mission Beach who respond to high winds in much the same way I do to fire. However,

I stay because I know that even if we experience a massive cyclone here, and I lost everything, this community will work together and support each other to get through it. I have stayed despite quite a few cyclone warnings.

A personal phenomenon I have noticed is that no matter how intense the previous few weeks' weather may have been in the region, when I eventually wake up to a glorious sunny morning, it is as though the previous bleak days had never happened.

'The Beach'

I love walking along the beach. The warmth of the sun and the feel of the water on my bare feet and legs is heavenly. Early morning: energy high, attempting a personal best for distance and time. Late afternoon: the soft breeze flits across my face as toes glide through the sand. A small wave pushes into shore and my feet sink slowly into the tepid water. Bliss!

There are 14 kms of the Mission Beach shoreline always waiting for me. Sometimes I walk down there from home, just for the challenge of 'the hill' on the way back to the house. When it is about the walk, not the exercise, I drive down, park and randomly select a pathway to enter. Should I turn left or should I turn right towards South Mission? Occasionally, if I have turned right, and the tide is out enough for me to cross the creek, I continue on until I reach a local cafe. Then I find I can't resist the enticing call of hot chips.

Often I take my camera and then it is not even about the walk.

As the weeks passed in Mission Beach, and the months turned into years, I looked back and saw much of the tenseness I had arrived with was beginning to disappear. Something in me was moving forward. How could I not be affected by the environment?

'Bee Eaters'

I bought a new camera this week. Blame it on the pair of Rainbow Bee Eaters in the garden.

RJ has cleaned Lloyd's Canon EOS and replaced the internal batteries for me, but I am still having a problem using it, keeping it steady. It is no longer because I am filled with grief holding it, now it is simply too heavy for my hands to manage. Oblivious to the fact they were about to have a 135 mm lens aimed in their direction, the bee eaters flitted about together; landing on the vine support wire; taking off, teasing each other with flirty behaviour. Mesmerising. It turns out, the photos were as much about the new garden as the birds—but that is ok too.

I felt I was becoming a part of the environment.

'Masked Lapwing'

Well, I have seen a few possessively parochial people in my time, but the title for 'most intense residents' this year surely must go to the two Masked Lapwings (referred to locally as Plovers) that decided to nest in the centre of the vacant land between my place and No. 35. 'Come on guys! This block is mown every three weeks. How long do you plan on staying?'

I don't like to spy on my neighbours—well, I don't like to spy on anyone—but the Lapwing next door appears to be sitting on eggs. Deleece, who lives on the other side, and I have been monitoring the situation. Today, while I was volunteering at the Mission Beach Visitors Information Centre next door to the C4 Environmental headquarters, I asked some of the Mission Beach Wildcare people if they could go out and check on the Dunkalli Crescent situation. Exciting news! They have confirmed there are two eggs in the nest. The Lapwing pair go nuts when any vehicles pull into our driveways. Good luck Michael when you decide to mow.

Several weeks later, after much anticipation, we have two chicks. Newly hatched, they are sending their parents even crazier than before. One chick heads down the hill; the other struggles up the hill. The 'baby being killed' noise, which could sometimes be confused with a city jackhammer, emanating from the over-anxious mum and dad is deafening. Michael can mow the lawn now. The family have moved to more forested parts.

I stayed because of the people

The afternoon my sister Margaret and I drove into Mission Beach, we had no intention of turning off the Bruce Highway before we reached Cairns. Our destination was Port Douglas and we had avoided any of the scenic temptations off Highway since we had departed my soon-to-be-sold Gold Coast home. Fifty metres past the Tully turnoff, I made a split-second decision and did a U turn back to the T intersection, then headed towards the coast.

What an incredibly beautiful drive it was through the rainforest that late afternoon, with the sun still filtering fiercely through the trees. When we reached the 80 km speed sign, I lowered the car windows and we breathed in fragrant tropical air.

Twenty-six kilometres later I pulled the car up outside the village green, turned off the engine and we stepped out onto the pavement. Margaret looked around her and said, "This is so you!"

"What do you mean?"

"Look around you—there's only a few parked cars, no traffic, no high-rise buildings and the people we can see are actually talking to each other. They look friendly. They're not taking any notice of us! There's wide blue sky and I can see plenty of blue water." I conceded that what I was seeing was 'very me' and Margaret suggested instead of continuing on, we stay the night. Have a look around to see if there were any suitable places for sale. After all, that was what this mad trip to Port Douglas was all about. "Mind you," she said as we walked towards the post office, "I couldn't live here. But I would come and visit you!"

I spent my first two years in Mission Beach renovating and bringing the house I had purchased up to building code. The only plant growing on the block of land was a struggling frangipani. The landscaping consisted of mounds of building rubble. Every time it rained, water ran down from the vacant land to the right of my place scouring the dirt, racing past the pool and under the lower verandah space.

Margaret and I had fallen in love with the house the moment we walked inside. It was obvious it was going to need a lot of work to bring out its potential—as the real estate people say—but neither of us was daunted. I had built, renovated, upgraded and decorated a few homes in the past. She was confident I could do it again.

As it turned out, the place was in a far worse state than we had been led to believe. We realised too late we should perhaps have flown in an independent building inspector instead of relying on a local. We discovered that not one appliance in the house worked: the lights were on but nothing actually happened. There had obviously been a significant electrical storm at some point before we purchased, as none of the pool equipment, garage door, stove, air conditioner, dishwasher—to name but a few—were usable. Electrical wiring wasn't to code.

We were pretty annoyed, but as the months went by, I realised there was actually a positive side. Margaret was in Canberra, but I was living and talking to the people in Mission, getting to know about the community I had moved into. If the place had been without problems, I would never have had the privilege of meeting some interesting tradies and the wives who ran the businesses. Compared to my previous building and renovating experiences, this proved to be painfully slow work. I eventually overcame my initial frustration at the length of time it took to get anything started here, let alone finished. There is something wholesome in a strange way to know your tradie isn't available this week because the fish are running. Many people I knew during my career worked outrageous hours in the hope they could retire to a lifestyle similar to what men and women already have here in this Region.

Good neighbours make a huge difference in how well one settles into a new community. I have some of the best. In fact, I am sure the good humour and friendship offered to me when I first arrived not only helped me settle in quickly, it also made me feel like staying.

It was through my neighbours I was able to source appropriate trades, get supplies in, get work done. Due to my last renovation project, I had strong contacts down south, but they weren't going to travel to Far North Queensland for a house upgrade. Thanks to the enthusiasm of Ollie and Michael to put things right, everything began to take shape. The people I met through them then introduced me to other trades.

My neighbours are good fun. They have been very kind to me over the years and we have shared more than a few laughs. One afternoon the first year I was in Mission Beach, Jerry asked me if I had been out to King Reef. 'No' I said, 'Tell me about it.' The next weekend, having monitored the timing of the extreme low tide, I was one of a group of lemmings cautiously making their way from the shore to the Reef almost a kilometre away. It was obvious everyone was conscious of the fragility of the Reef. We walked in the shoe sucking mud of course, not on the Reef itself. I was keeping a close eye on the time, as I didn't want to be caught out there when the tide turned and the water rose. Jerry had said the water wouldn't get above ankle deep, so I wore my rolled-up jeans. I was almost there, water already to my thighs, when I heard my name called out by Jerry.

'I thought you said this water remained ankle deep!' I yelled across to him.

'Well I sort of guessed that bit' he yells back. 'This is Liz's and my first time out here too! I guess it's ankle deep if you are tall.'

My sons and their families have quite intense lives and I rarely see them in person these days. One of the great joys I have experienced in Mission Beach has been my inclusion into the family life of some of my younger friends. One delightful pre-schooler took it into her head to call me Grandma. As all of her grandparents live overseas, and my granddaughter's interstate, it was a lovely feeling to hear that name applied to me and to receive warm hugs whenever we met. Another neighbour used to bring her children across to have a swim, while we chatted over a coffee. She eventually moved south to take up a work position, but they come and see me whenever they return to visit their relatives who live in the region.

I stayed because I can do as much or as little as I want

When I recently read over some of the earlier pieces I had written for the boys in my Blog, I could see the beneficial effect Mission Beach and its natural environment was having on me. At first I was intoxicated by the sheer beauty of the area and that was reflected in the words and photographs I posted. Then I noticed a subtle difference creeping into the tone of my writing. I became more relaxed and a little introspective. In Darwin it is said that one lives on Territory time, not real time. Dare I say, I began to live on Mission Beach time.

There is something incredibly comfortable in allowing oneself to sit on a verandah, looking out towards the Great Barrier Reef at any time of day: perhaps sharing a drink and food with friends or, as Darryl Kerrigan said in the iconic Australian movie "The Castle", simply taking in the serenity. It is magic.

'Chilling'

After weeks of busyness, literally getting things done while the sun was shining, today I find myself chilling out with a cup of coffee and doing nothing in particular. A misty rain is falling; not tropical strength, but enough to hide the reef from my view. I am the first to admit I prefer to relax in warm sunshine, but there is a visual softness to this type of day.

Sunday afternoons such as this promote a series of coulds or shoulds in my mind. I could finish making the cushion covers, I could pay accounts today instead of tomorrow, I could cook a date loaf or I could run that stuff down to our version of the Green Shed [a recycling complex in Canberra]. Then I look out the window again and think, nah, it can all wait. This is definitely an afternoon for procrastinating.

'Embracing the Cold Afternoon'

The sun broke through around midday—but the day remained chilly, notwithstanding the blue skies. The wind died down though and sitting out on the deck seemed like a good idea for Sunday afternoon.

I dragged out the trackie daks and a fleece jumper, then looked for my short Ugg boots. Even pulled a rug from the cupboard. Armed with a mug of hot soup, I made my way outside and sat back in the 'egg' chair to read my book. The hours have flown by. I am feeling cosy and contented. I have enjoyed this afternoon very much. One hundred per cent lazy, one hundred per cent happy. Cold air on my face has brought my attention back to the real world. The golden glow of the setting sun on the tall palms is good to see once again. The swallows have been swooping and circling as the evening sounds begin to break through. I know I should return to the warmth of the house, start my evening meal, but I am strangely reluctant to move.

I stayed because of the creative opportunities

Trudy Tschui, our local councillor, introduced me to many local people and suggested I would enjoy involvement with Mission Arts. She was correct. Who would have known that a small village contained so many talented people? Mission Arts Gallery and Shop recently celebrated its tenth anniversary. Planning began for the gallery in 2010, and building had just commenced when—you've guessed it—Cyclone Yasi hit. Words alone cannot describe the damage this Category 5 cyclone caused. Last year I put together an audio-visual presentation for the anniversary awards night, 'Ten Years from 2011 to 2021'— and my respect for the original Mission Arts management committee, who somehow got themselves back up on their feet and rebuilt, is huge. The original building frame had just gone up in February, then it was destroyed, steel twisted beyond recognition. Despite having to remove stripped leaf litter and similar vegetation from the site—photos indicate it reached the height of a two-storey building—the project was completed and handed over to the original committee by the end of August the same year. What an achievement for a small village that had literally been blown away.

My initial contact with Mission Arts was when I tried out a mosaic workshop held at the Gallery. Thanks to Annie, I later became involved with the Mission Arts Management Committee and various sub committees. Despite intending to pursue a somewhat isolated lifestyle when I first moved to Mission Beach, so I could concentrate on my writing, I quickly became absorbed into the busy Arts Community.

Mission Arts provides an opportunity for people living in and around Mission Beach to both enjoy and participate in all areas of the visual arts. Classes and workshops are held regularly, catering right through from the novice to the professional artist. Mission Beach has its own pottery shed and also a glass kiln. Opening nights for Exhibitions become an exciting time. The above mentioned Tenth Anniversary Awards event was a lot of fun. Before the night was over, even I was on my feet dancing to the live music. There is a great sense of satisfaction in seeing local work adorn the walls and standing proud on plinths. Mission Arts is run 100% on volunteer labour, so to achieve the standards it does is quite an achievement.

Mission Beach also offers opportunities for local members of Licualawinq Writers to meet and mentor each other on the last Sunday of each month. We don't always meet at the Beach, but at a variety of venues in the region where we enjoy brunch with a side serve of story telling. Discovering a group of people who, like me, actually love to write has reawakened my passion for words.

The abundance of creative opportunities is yet another reason why I have stayed in Mission Beach. Given the small size of the local population, it is truly refreshing to find such a focus on so many aspects of creative lifestyles.

I stayed because of the community spirit

My favourite community based activity is working as a Volunteer at the Visitors [Tourism] Information Centre. With house and garden improvements well under way, I began to make an effort to explore the natural attractions surrounding my new home. I found myself wanting to know more details about the areas I was visiting, so I kept making my way down to the Visitors Information Centre in Porter Promenade. One day it was suggested I join their team and become a volunteer myself. The idea appealed to me, so I did. It was one of the best decisions I have made in Mission Beach.

Introducing visitors to the local attractions, directing them to local businesses and sharing their excitement and anticipation as they set out to see the region reminds me each week of how much the area has to offer. I become aware again of one of the reasons I have chosen to stay here. Tourism is really the lifeblood of the village and it is good to be able to promote that for our local people. Many of the VIC volunteers help out in other areas of the community too. My experience has been that the hours of volunteering I put in come back to me many times over—often in the form of fun friendships—but also in knowing I have contributed something towards making Mission Beach the place I want to stay.

'Cassowaries'

The question we get asked most often at the Visitors Information Centre is 'Where can we see a cassowary?' We reply appropriately and remind our visitors to slow or stop if they see a cassowary on or near the road, and under no circumstances to try feeding them. A family came in a few weeks ago, pleased to be holidaying in Mission Beach and all ready for some adventures. We answered their cassowary questions and told them where they might see one in the national park. Several hours later the family returned to the VIC. The kids ran in bursting with excitement, telling us they had seen a cassowary. Their dad said they were so happy about the sighting they wanted to come back and tell the ladies in the Centre. Wasn't that sweet?

I stayed despite a *few* environmental problems

Three years ago, I was one of several people in the area to suffer the effects of a white tailed rat invasion. Yes, I know they are 'cute' natives, but you will see why they are not my favourites. As I had no idea these particular creatures existed, it came as a bit of a shock when faced with their destruction. I woke up around 2 am to the sound of running water. It took a moment or two before I realised it wasn't raining. I thought maybe a washer had gone on the tap over the laundry tub, so headed down the stairs. As I stepped onto the floor, feeling for the light switch, I realised I was standing up to my ankles in water.

The light revealed water pouring from various parts of the ceiling: through the down lights, through the fans, across the beams—you get the picture. For a moment my mind went blank, then I realised the pipes in the ceiling had burst. As I didn't have the strength to turn the water off at the mains, I reluctantly phoned my neighbour Jerry. (At first he thought it was his alarm going off, then Liz thought it was hers). He came across, but this being Mission Beach of course the mains water tap had rusted tight. Jerry had to return home and get some serious gear to stop the water. Have I mentioned how wonderful my neighbours are? Anyway, it turned out white tailed rats had come in and chewed through the water pipes.

The damage was appalling. Drying walls; demolishing furniture; tearing out; tossing out; trying to salvage precious papers and historical books; dealing with the insurance company and its sub-contractors. I discovered shortcuts the original builder had taken. I spent months washing everything by hand because the washing machine had been destroyed; waiting months for a replacement machine, then discovering that it was faulty; waiting for another one to be ordered and delivered. The rebuilding and the repainting seemed to take forever. If ever anything was going to make me leave Mission Beach, that event would have been it.

The positive was that I again got to see the best side of people in the village.

Two other environmental problems that I encountered, typical in the tropics, were green tree ants and feral pigs. I wasn't sure if I should tell the boys about the ants, but wrote about them anyway.

'Green Tree Ants'

OK. So I have this problem with green tree ants. Due to the amount of research I have done lately, I can tell you they are also called weaver ants and live in colonies of 200,000 plus per nest. Everyone has green tree ants in the tropics. It's a given. They are cute and helpful (and even tasty according to a chef I know) BUT - somehow I have made my garden too inviting. There are no longer just a few leafy colonies occupying a shrub or two. No—I have a total 'take over the world and take no prisoners' infestation. When I attempt to pluck limes from one of my fruit trees, I wear a swimming costume under a raincoat in case the ant attack requires me to jump in the swimming pool. That has worked quite well in the past, and the fruit grabbed has been worth an unscheduled dip, but lately these guys have upped the ante. That tree and those limes have become a battle ground.

On a recent FaceTime chat with Margaret [my sister] she told me how she had dealt with green tree ants invading her place when she lived in Darwin. The Territory pest man at first said 'We don't usually worry about green tree ants unless they're a problem'. Margaret's response was 'I think finding them in my bed on the first floor IS a problem'. He then explained how to get nests into buckets of water. This subsequently worked well for her: she thought I should give it a go.

Yes. Well. I felt so confident this would work I didn't change into my swimmers or raincoat. I left the hat off my head. It was late afternoon, going on early evening, and there was no sign of ant activity. I moved in with the long cutters, buckets of water already in situ. First cut—first yell. I struggled to cut the first nest free of its tethers, but it did finally drop into a bucket. Suddenly two billion ants appear from nowhere.

They have run up the handles of the loppers and are running up and down my arms onto my body. I am determined they won't stop me. I aim for the next nest. Ants are running at an alarming speed along every tree branch. Suddenly they launch an aerial attack. My hair is full of stinging, biting green tree ants. That's it. I drop the loppers. I start to remove my shirt and shorts before I have hit the laundry door. I fly up the stairs and jump in the shower, water running through my hair for ten minutes in an effort to rid myself of the bitey little critters.

I haven't picked a fresh lime in over a week.

When you live in an area such as the Wet Tropics, you have to expect a few issues with the 'locals'. The problems caused by feral pigs in this area, however, I feel fall into another category altogether. Therefore, I won't mention my battle with feral pigs except to say my previous lawn area will probably be ready for planting with sugar cane by the end of the month.

I have stayed because I like to challenge myself on behalf of the environment

'Gardening Past and Present'

My four-year-old self used to follow Dad around our Sydney garden early every morning. He would tend his roses, pick fresh mandarins from our tree, check on his bean crop and so on, all before he got ready for work in the CBD.

I know my deep interest in gardening came from this shared time with him. He was quite knowledgeable, but never afraid to ask those who knew more than he did for advice. One of his real joys was to get out of his office at Circular Quay and spend most weekday lunchtimes talking to the gardeners in the Royal Botanical Gardens. He would eat the sandwiches Mum had lovingly prepared for him, while he chatted to the men and women who had great passion for the gardens they developed and maintained.

Due to my erratic career and lifestyle choices, it wasn't until I married Lloyd that I had my own garden to tend. As he expressed it, he bought a house with an aircraft hangar so he could garage his purple and black V8 Torana. (Yes—really, it had housed small aeroplanes and we lived opposite an airport. And, to be fair, the Torana sported two aircraft landing lights on the front bumper bar for driving through the Central West at night). On the front 'lawn' was one lonely, struggling stick of a wattle tree. That was the total contribution to landscaping. This plant didn't even reach knee level.

Before he knew it, that newly married man was buying railway sleepers and mulch and discovering what was beyond the gates of the local Council Nursery. He found out that if you buy a garden hose and use it, the wattle stick soon becomes a glorious tree of vivid yellow fluff. Plant some grevilleas around the entire house and hey presto! The blossoms are a stunning display of pinks and creams and crimsons. They grew so well he had to cut out a space for the electricity meter reader to walk through. When we moved on, we sold the place to a retired farmer's wife who also loved to garden.

Our five acres at Wamboin, which was situated 900 metres above sea level at the headwaters of the Yass River, was about 100 metres outside the ACT/NSW border. Our hilltop was in a direct line with Black Mountain and shared the same ecological features. We never meant the acreage to be more than a natural environment in which our sons could enjoy some of the freedoms we both had as children. In fact, we used to refer to the block as 'Little Namadgi'. After a few years, however, thanks to a bio recycled reticulating water system we had installed, we had a delightful lawn and flower beds surrounding the house itself; a herb garden at the back. I grew lots of roses and lavender; annuals like pansies and petunias; straw covered beds hiding tulip bulbs; tubs of irises; hyacinths and violets growing wild. In Spring the hillsides were covered in wildflowers and the birdlife was prolific. Occasionally, people from CSIRO and ANU came out to unofficially catalogue the block. When it was purchased in 2007, the two ornithologists who bought it from us put a legally binding wildlife protection covenant on the block.

I truly loved my acreage and garden and it brought us all so much pleasure. Brother-in-law John showed the boys how to collect seeds and after we had the boundaries ripped, he planted these out with them. Most grew successfully. My eldest son became a keen environmentalist as he grew up. He was responsible as a child for discovering when the local green organisations had plants available. Over the years he planted trays and trays of seedlings. Today these also create a beautiful display. He understood his mother's and grandfather's delight in the fragrance of a perfect rose bloom. When I couldn't dig through the shale to plant a new variety, he would come and help me. I am so very pleased that he has his own acreage in Virginia now with his own rose gardens.

During my years on the Gold Coast I renovated my parent's suburban garden, which had been overrun by creepers and damaged by falling palm fronds since my father had died. The landscaping outcome was crisp and attractive, but my heart was never in it like it had been at Wamboin.

I have lived in Darwin, but that experience didn't really prepare me at all for gardening in the Tropics. Lloyd and I lived in a double storied, stand alone townhouse in Garden Hills— very close to the Darwin Botanical Gardens. It had modern courtyard gardens, which had been planted and manicured to within an inch of their lives. It was lovely. So lovely we were joined every night by a family of possums who also enjoyed our lifestyle. Leave a pizza box on the table and by the time you returned with a cold drink, the box was half empty.

Relocating to Mission Beach I thought my gardening days were over. Little did I know what delights awaited me.

When faced with erosion problems, over time I have found a plant/vegetation solution works best, provided appropriate structural and drainage issues are addressed. Prevention is always better than trying to find a remedial solution. It was the need to prevent further damage that had me asking Brian, a local landscaping nurseryman, to help me design and then construct an environmentally friendly garden. Between us, with his knowledge of tropical plants, and my knowledge of Australian natives, we managed over time to develop a sound, if somewhat hybrid garden.

I am the first to admit I am not as young as I once was, and cannot do as much physically as I would like. However, with a little external help, this garden has matured and now provides me with a great deal of aesthetic pleasure. The native plants attract an incredible array of bird life and also provide sun shelter for the visiting Agile wallabies. It is still difficult to grasp the fact that after a day or two of heavy rain, yesterday's weed free garden bed is again dense with those pesky plants. Or that the well-behaved ginger by the pool has grown several metres overnight and now touches the top deck. I have had to be ruthless in cutting out some non-native domestic plants. I can't afford to lose sight of the fact that these can, in the wrong climate, become an out of control environmental crisis.

My garden isn't quite an old friend yet, but we are getting to know each other better.

Why do other people stay in Mission Beach?

As I have been writing this, reflecting on why I have stayed in Mission Beach, it has made me think about why the people I interact with every day have stayed here. Some of my neighbours, for example, have lived in Mission Beach for many years. These people have survived cyclones Larry and Yasi; they suffered varying degrees of material loss, but rebuilt their lives and businesses and still enjoy living here. Others are relative newcomers: some have been here longer than me, some are recent arrivals.

I decided the best way to find out was to ask some of them directly why they have stayed in Mission Beach: to see if their experience was similar to mine.

My friend Janet works with me at the Visitors Information Centre and is also a neighbour. When I asked her, she sent me this: 'I am sitting on my verandah listening to the rain. Earlier I could hear the ocean, but the rain has drowned out that sound. Everything is green and bright and glistening. There is only a small part of one other house in sight. A wallaby wandered through a few minutes ago and I am often visited by a cassowary and his chick. There is a lake at the bottom of my garden. The lake does have a resident crocodile, but he minds his own business and he looks so regal as he swims past with that long sweeping tail. There is only one place I know with that combination.'

Jerry and Liz were working in their garden when I asked them.

"Definitely the climate," says Jerry. "The consistent climate." For Liz it was a range of things. "Definitely environmental. That is really important. Living in a small community." As we speak a colourful Cairns Birdwing butterfly brazenly flits between us. "As I was saying," continues Liz, "It is the stunning environment we live in. The natural world around us. I have strong family connections going back generations too. Our history goes a long way back in this area and, of course, it is the small community itself. It all adds up to why we stay."

Carol and Richard have been in Mission Beach a long time: 37 years.

"We came down from Cairns originally because we were overseeing a new business venture. The one month we had allowed ourselves suddenly turned into twelve months. At some point we realised we didn't want to return to Cairns. Mission Beach was busier then, not the same as today. It had almost all we wanted. We were enjoying the lifestyle. We still do. We threw ourselves into community organisations, the same as we had done in Cairns. Our son and his family live here and they and their friends are very happy with no foreseeable plans to leave. It is a great community to live in."

I asked Barb and Faye while we were volunteering at the Mission Beach Markets, setting up a Tourism Information desk on Sunday. For Faye, her business interests initially kept her in Mission Beach. Now it is her family and friends and the community itself. "After 32 years," she says, "I am passionate about the area."

"For me," said Barb, "the better question is why do I keep coming back? I think I keep coming back to Mission Beach because it feels more like home than anywhere else we have lived in Australia. The sense of community here is very strong. It's where my son grew up. This is the fourth time we have returned. The Mission Beach community creates a sense of belonging, no matter where you came from or whoever you are."

So it seems that whatever brought or led us here in the first place, it is the magic of the environment and the integrity of the community itself in Mission Beach that keeps us all here.

In conclusion

It is said that life is cyclic; somewhere there is a beginning, and somewhere an end; but ultimately towards that end we may find ourselves somewhere close to where we began.

I shared this story with the boys a couple of years ago.

'Coincidence'

Life is full of coincidences, but sometimes one of these events is worthy of mention. I just had one of those moments, so here I am hitting the keyboard to tell you all about it.

I've come across an old tourist envelope with 'Cooktown' printed on the outside. Inside is a letter written to Mum and Dad from Lloyd and I - written this week exactly forty years ago! [1980]. We were younger than you are now.

Lloyd: "When we started our holiday we didn't think we would end up so far north, but boy are we lad we did. It is marvellous. I think if it was at all possible we would keep going north. ..."

So forty years later, here I am back in the Wet Tropics, still in love with the mountains and the reef, the cane fields and the bananas. Sadly, of course, Lloyd is no longer with me, but there are times I get the feeling he may not be so far away after all.

No wonder I have stayed. This is the area we commenced our life's journey together in August 1980.

My Life is Tully

By Jean Vallianos

I was born in Innisfail during the early part of World War Two and, aside from a few short years in the nearby town of Silkwood, have lived most of my eight decades in Tully.

I attended Tully State Primary School and sat for the Junior, or leaving certificate, in 1957. I had to leave school and get a job to support my mother and brother. I worked first for a solicitor and then the Commonwealth Bank. During those years I studied by correspondence for my Senior certificate, the equivalent of today's Year 12, and then Accounting. I attained my Certified Practising Accountant (CPA) qualification, which helped set me up for life ahead.

Life has always had its challenges. In 1961 I helped my mother (who could not speak English) run the Red Hill Grocery Store, which we took over when the owner left. I knew nothing about running a shop and still remember being asked for Rothman cigarettes and having no idea what they were. I learnt they were a very popular brand of cigarettes. My mother made free cups of coffee and biscuits for everyone. We all loved her.

She wanted me to go to Greece to meet a young man to be my husband even though many local Greek men wanted to marry me. However, I met Nick at dance in 1956 and it was love at first sight. He kept asking me to marry him but I had to convince my mother and brother he was the one I really wanted. We were not allowed to go out on our own and I thank God that we were both persistent and our love endured. We both made sure we met at church and

Greek dances. Finally, I am happy to say, my brother and mother agreed with my choice and we were married in 1966.

I could have left when my father died. An uncle said we could stay with him in Brisbane. We stayed here, in Tully. If I had left to go to university, who knows, I might never have met Nick. I stayed and have no regrets.

Over the years we had to cope with cyclones, floods, business competition and health problems. However, we stayed. Despite all, Nick and I had a wonderful life. We had two girls and a boy and even when they grew up and had to go to Townsville to university we stayed. When they got married and left Tully for good, we stayed. When Nick died, my girls and son asked me to stay with them but I stayed here.

WHY?

I love my family, the people, the whole community. They all know me, and my family. I helped on many committees, taking on many office bearer positions—Chairman, Vice-Chairman, Secretary, Treasurer. Blue Nurses, Nursing Home, Red Cross, Country Women's Association (CWA), Chamber of Commerce etc, etc. I have mentored others to take on these positions too.

We have a multicultural society with Aboriginal people, English, Scottish, Irish, New Zealanders, Italian, Greek, Yugoslav, and others from European countries, and now from India, China, Japan, Indonesia, Korea, Vietnam, South Africa and South America. There are too many to remember. We all get on together and respect each other's culture.

I have not mentioned the unique beauty of the mountains, the rainforest, the fauna and flora of the Cassowary Coast. Tully is in the valley nestled between Mt Tyson, Mt Mackay, and the Walter Hill and Kirrima ranges. It is the home of the cassowary, cockatoos, wallabies, and possums, many species of birds and butterflies, especially the Ulysses or Blue Mountain butterfly. I could go on about our trees, our orchids and our plants that are all unique to this area. We may be the wettest town in Australia but without the rain we would have nothing.

Tully is situated half-way between Cairns and Townsville and only 15 minutes from the loveliest beaches of North/South Mission, and those beaches near the mouths of the Tully and Hull rivers. Marine life abounds and we can visit the islands and reefs just off the beaches. We have natural swimming holes and the World Rafting Championships were held at Tully Gorge in 2019.

There is so much here to see and do, why would I want to leave? To me, this is Paradise. I want to stay.

Contributors

Sarah Board was born in Sydney, is 24, and a fifth generation Australian. She is described as a constantly smiling, bubbly, and giggly young woman who loves anything creative. She looks for any way or form to express herself. She either does it, or it's on her list of to do's. She is always looking for an adventure. Sarah is new to the world of writing and *Magic Carpet Ride* is her first published work. Currently she is working on a novel as a hobby.

Barbara Bufi is 86 years young and has been Cosmo's widow for 29 years. Born in Townsville, she came to Innisfail when she was four. She was educated at Sacred Heart Convent Innisfail, and Lourdes Hill in Brisbane. She was the first assistant librarian in the Innisfail Library in 1952 and in 1955 married Cosmo, an El Arish cane farmer. Two sons and two daughters were born during their 17 years on the farm. In the 70s Cosmo and Barbara bought a mixed business where Barbara was postmistress of East Innisfail Post Office. After leaving the post office they moved to the top of the hill where Barbara still resides more than 50 years later. Her children live nearby and she rejoices in seven grandchildren who this year presented her with three great-grandies. She now has to read from a screen and misses the smell and feel of a new book, but the words she devours daily are food for her soul. Though her life and activities are winding down, Barbara maintains active membership of Licualawinq, Women Writers Queensland, and the Flying Fish Point branch of Queensland Country Women's Association.

Jacque Duffy is best known for her award-winning artwork. She is also a published author/illustrator of books for children, articles, short stories and poetry. She lives in the rainforests of Tropical North Queensland, Australia, where she is kept busy creating art and working on her first novel length work.

Penelope Goward was born in Adelaide in 1952. She moved to Melbourne in her mid-twenties to continue her nursing qualifications, including midwifery and community health nursing. Needing a change, she did a degree in Computing, and gained a Master of Education, and later completed a PhD in cross-cultural research. Education, writing, and editing have been consistent across her mixed careers in nursing, IT, teaching at university level, and teaching English in China to teachers. Penelope writes in the non-fiction area and has been published in a women's journal, academic journals, and written many business and education documents. She also reads widely. Penelope moved to Mission Beach after retiring and discovered Licualawinq.

Santina Lizzio was born in the Innisfail District Hospital and has remained a permanent resident of the Cassowary Coast Region since then. She has written several books on local history and published a complete collection of her poems and short stories. Her keen interest in military animals of war has earned her acknowledgement from the Australian Defence Force Trackers and War Dogs Association. Many of her military poems are used around Australia at various military services.

Bruce G Lowe was born and raised in Innisfail. He has explored most of the far north and endured direct hits by three severe tropical cyclones all while resisting the temptation to grow webs between his toes despite the rain. His family began a business there in 1928, which continues to this day. He is passionate about many things such as writing poetry, short stories, working on his first novel, as well as travelling the world, growing rare palms, and his wife.

Brenda May arrived in the tropical North from Adelaide in 1981 on a working holiday and never left. After five years on Dunk Island and three years at the tip of Cape York, Brenda settled in Japoonvale, started her family, and ran a wildlife tour business with her partner for 20 years. Now living in Innisfail, Brenda is a romance suspense author, working on a six-book series called '*All Roads Lead to Love*'. The first book, '*A Wild Ride to Love*', was released this year. The second book, '*A Hostage to Love*' is well on its way to completion. Brenda's head is full of thoughts and ideas. She is also working on a fantasy series, '*The Dragon Dreams*', and has numerous children's stories wanting to be told.

Cassandra Smith is a refugee writer from the fringes of the 90s music scene in Brisbane who came to teach in the far north of Queensland in 2008. She is married with a daughter, two cats, two guinea pigs and five chickens. She endeavours to teach students how to better express themselves and scribbles in her spare time.

Jeannette Smith was gifted the largest dictionary her son and his wife could find for her 50th birthday. She could barely lift it. "Just in case," they said, "you have begun to run out of words. You do know everyone has 860,341,500 words inside them. They use them up, then they die. We are giving you more words!" Ten years later her sons set up a blog for her to keep in touch with everyone "so we see your photographs and get to read what we haven't got time to listen to on the phone". After spending decades in many places, writing, editing, typing for others, she feels the time has come to write for herself and thanks her family and friends for their persistent encouragement, and Mission Beach for making her feel welcome.

Laurie Ross Trott was raised in Cairns when kids paddled tin canoes in flooded streets and looked forward to fireworks on Guy Fawkes night. Aged 10, her 'poem' extolling the wonders of Bungalow Bakery bread won a family pass to the Coral Drive-In cinema. Her writing future was cast in dough. A journalist, she has worked in Sydney, Perth, Port Headland, and regional Queensland. Curtin University awarded her First Class Honours in

Screen Arts. Her poetry is published in print and online. Her play 'To Kill A Cassowary' premiered in Cairns in 2020 and is published by Playlab Theatre.

Jean Vallianos OAM is 81 years old and still loves writing. At 12, she won an Anzac essay competition for children under 16 and it was read out at Anzac services. Over the next 60 years her family—Nick, Dorothea, Vaitsa, Gerasimos, and friends read her essays and poems, but it wasn't till she joined Licualawinq writers that she shared with others. Along with her Order of Australia Medal she has received many awards, including the Rotary Paul Harris, Cassowary Coast Citizen of the year 2012, and Life Memberships of Red Cross and Tully Nursing Home. She loves her community and looks to see what she can do to help make it the best place to live.

(Facilitator) Ken Allen's name should be Jack, he is a master of all trades, and he can even fly a helicopter. Author of the popular novels *'All That's Left'*, and *'ASIO Exposed'*, under the name K A Allen. Ken keeps himself busy working as a photographer and drone pilot/cinematographer.

9 780645 031348